PROFITABLE SELLING

Profitable Selling

JOHN LIDSTONE

Wildwood House

First published in hardback 1977 by Gower Press, Teakfield Ltd
under the title *Negotiating Profitable Sales*

Reprinted 1980, 1981 by Gower Publishing Company Limited

This paperback edition published 1986 by
Wildwood House Limited
Gower House
Croft Road
Aldershot
Hampshire GU11 3HR
England

British Library Cataloguing in Publication Data

Lidstone, John, 1929–
   [Negotiating profitable sales]. Profitable Selling.
   1. Selling
   I. [Negotiating profitable sales].   II. Title
   658.8'5   HF5438.25

ISBN 0 7045 0524 X

Printed and bound in Great Britain by
Biddles Ltd, Guildford and King's Lynn

Contents

Tables

Figures

Preface

Selling has traditionally been seen as the process through which the individual salesman persuades the individual buyer to purchase goods, services or ideas. For many years salesmen and saleswomen have been trained in a wide variety of techniques of persuasive communication to carry out this process effectively and efficiently.

But the market environment in which selling takes place is changing very rapidly and will continue to do so. The characteristics of the market place in which consumer, industrial and service companies operate have been changed dramatically in the last ten years by the emergence and growth of the big buyer. More and more commercial and industrial organisations are becoming dominated by fewer and fewer companies. Takeovers and mergers bear ample testimony to this development and there are some notable and well-publicised examples influencing our personal and business lives, from banking and insurance to the giant chemical and food manufacturers, supermarketing chains, and the local and national newspapers.

These purchasers of your products, services, processes and ideas face more complex and competitive conditions in their markets. This has resulted in your major customers becoming more complex to sell to, more demanding, more professional in their approach to buying and in buying methods and above all more financially aware of the importance and effect of each buying decision they reach and make with their suppliers.

Some of you may deplore this development and concentration of buying power and wish that your company could opt out and deal with the still small independent businesses. But you cannot put the clock back. These buyers of your products and services who are larger in size but fewer in number represent for many suppliers over seventy per cent of their business. So the defection of only one of these key customers can be costly not just in volume but in the overall profitability of your company.

Because such customers are the cornerstones of prosperity, of profit and of your own selling job, you need much more than basic selling techniques to survive and compete successfully for worthwhile business now and in the years ahead.

The advanced salesman must be skilled not only in the art of selling but also in the techniques of handling these professional larger buyers.

He has to operate in this changed market place against ever-increasing national and international competition and at a time when costs and prices are changing constantly and rapidly due to worldwide inflation and energy and commodity shortages.

Purpose of this workbook

This workbook has been compiled to help the advanced salesman to develop his or her knowledge and skill in three key areas:

First. How to understand the financial aspects of his work in relation to major customers. In a world of constantly changing costs and prices salesmen must be capable of ensuring not only that an order is obtained but that it is a profitable one. This workbook will show how to use financial knowledge and techniques in selling to these bigger buyers.

Second. How to prepare in far more detail than has been done before strategies for each major customer and planning how to set about this task so that all the resources of the company can be harnessed to achieve short- and long-term customer satisfaction at a profit.

Third. How to negotiate with these major customers to the point of obtaining a mutually satisfactory order and long-term business rather than just using persuasive techniques for the occasional 'your turn this time round' type of order. Many of these major buyers have no option but to purchase from the major supplier. But the key to success is the terms on which the contract to trade is agreed.

Who should use it?

This workbook is written for three groups of people: first, for all salesmen and saleswomen who sell to key-account major buyers, although their title may range from managing director, salesman to merchandiser. For them this book is designed as a self-teaching manual and practical source of reference when planning major selling calls. For sales managers and marketing managers who have the responsibility of managing these key-account salesmen this book will, I hope, provide a practical means of developing their own and their salesmen's skills in planning, in finance and in sales negotiation.

For the sales training manager it is designed to provide a practical basis and source of material for developing negotiating skills and as a training manual in conjunction with Chapter 11, Developing negotiating skills.

Content of this book

This workbook has been constructed in two parts:

Part One examines the market place in which the salesman operates and the changes that have led to the emergence of the larger companies and more professional buyers and the consequent necessity for the *new* knowledge, *skills*, *attitudes* and *expertise* salesmen need to operate successfully; the need for financial awareness in selling so that salesmen can direct their selling efforts towards the profits of their key customers and their own companies; the mechanism relating to costs and break-even in business.

Part Two concentrates on all the ingredients that are involved in negotiation: understanding the differences between negotiation and selling: buyer behaviour and motivation; planning negotiations, the strategy and tactics of negotiation; group presentations; and finally Chapter 11, providing line managers and sales training specialists with guidelines on how to approach the task of developing the negotiating skills of their key-account salesmen to the point of practical application on the job.

Throughout this workbook, planning formats, simple diagrams and illustrations will I hope enable the least numerate of sales staff to grasp the arithmetic of finance; and examples taken from real-life commercial situations will enable salesmen, sales trainers, sales national accounts managers, and negotiators in every type of business to use this book as a source of reference in planning successful and profitable negotiating for their customers and for their companies in the future.

John Lidstone

Marketing Improvements,
Ulster House,
Ulster Terrace,
Regent's Park,
London NW1

1977

Acknowledgements

It is the very essence of marketing consultancy that its concepts and techniques do not hit one between the eyes like a thunderbolt, but evolve over years to produce the desired result. For this reason it is impossible to acknowledge fully or adequately all the companies and present and past consultants who have contributed to the development of the approaches to negotiating profitable sales described in this book. While acknowledging my enormous debt to all these people throughout the world, I should like to single out a few and thank them individually for their help.

I would like to acknowledge the indebtedness of Marketing Improvements to:

Eric Atkins and his management colleagues in Lever Brothers and in the Van Den Bergh and United Agricultural Merchants' subsidiaries of Unilever.

Humfrey Smeeton, Managing Director of Cory Distribution, Subsidiary of Ocean Transport & Trading Ltd, for permission to reproduce financial ratios and a list of concessions.

David Money-Coutts, Chairman, and Julian Robarts, Deputy Managing Director, of Coutts & Co., Bankers, for many helpful conversations about the role of negotiation in the marketing of banking and financial services.

Michael Holliday, MIL's Director of UK Operations whose unerring farming instincts sniffed out some of the essential elements that differentiate negotiation from selling; to David Senton 'Director and General Manager, MI Europe, Brussels) and Peter Kirkby (Director, MI International Operations) whose negotiation taped case studies have become so well known as teaching aids. (The transcripts of these are reproduced in Chapter 5, 'Why Negotiation' and Chapter 10, 'Conduct of Negotiations'.)

Finally, I should like to thank my colleague and fellow author of *Managing a Sales Force*, Michael Wilson, for his contribution in two areas. His constructive criticisms have helped to improve many sections of this book. More important than this, he has built and inspired the talented Marketing Improvements team of which I am proud to be a member.

There is still much to record and learn about the arts and skills of negotiation, but I hope in some small way this book will stimulate, motivate and help all who negotiate to practise the art in the interests of satisfying their customers' and their companies' needs profitably.

John Lidstone

PART I
FINANCIAL TECHNIQUES IN SELLING

1 Selling today

The development of the 'marketing concept' approach to business – the creation of customers and keeping them satisfied profitably by finding out what they require and then making it, rather than by the traditional method of making things and then trying to sell them – has produced some revolutionary changes in the market place, in the attitudes of manufacturers to their customers and suppliers and in the role of the sales force.

But this customer-facing marketing concept – a new label for a very old recipe for commercial success, as blacksmiths, portrait painters and bespoke tailors will testify – however imaginatively and vigorously pursued no longer answers the problem of how to survive and prosper.

What one company decides to do can also be done by others. Modern technology, new materials and new inventions have enabled national and international companies not only to adopt the marketing concept, but to exploit the repertoire of marketing, production and distribution techniques available to all to provide custom-built products and services at prices people can afford and be persuaded to pay. The knowledge, skills and information among competing manufacturers large and small throughout the world today are similar. What one company spends millions of pounds, dollars or francs on over several years and invents today others can imitate tomorrow; so another fact of commercial life in this last quarter of the twentieth century which companies have to accept is that imitation is quicker and cheaper than invention and far less risky. Frequently companies even spurn to copy and instead take over the source of competitive inventions. Similarly, the costs companies incur in producing and distributing their products and services tend to be alike as are their ultimate selling prices to the buyer.

The marketing environment

The environment in which manufacturers, commercial and service companies operate and compete with each other is characterised by three factors.

1 Similarity of products and services

The products and services offered by competing companies tend to be similar if not frequently identical in appearance and advantages. In many markets, such as food, paper tissues and paint, a brand leader faces a similar product on an opposite shelf in supermarket, self-service and cash-and-carry outlets. Except that a twin has 'own-label' packaging, it is the same product, made by the same company. The same duplication is discernible in the basic design of mass-produced cars from Britain, Europe and Japan. In the electrical gadget field, the only difference between transistor radios, pocket calculators and tape recorders in similar price brackets is the manufacturer's name. Take the back off and all share a common origin and source of cheaply produced printed circuitry. The catalogue of identical products is endless, reflecting the age-old ability to imitate rather than to invent. Services such as banking, insurance and packaged holidays follow similar patterns.

2 Similarity in prices and discounts

The prices charged by companies for similar products and services also tend to be alike. New and/or demonstrably superior products and services are charged at a premium until a competitor enters the field and starts to encroach on sales. Then prices are reduced. The result is that with few notable exceptions the majority of products and services we buy – clothing, detergents, food, petrol, banking, insurance, estate agency – those offered by competing companies tend to be alike in product and service benefits and in the prices we pay for them or in the discounts we are allowed if we are the distributor. And this is true whether we are marketing in Lisbon or London, in Bangkok or Brussels, since multinational companies develop worldwide specifications for their products and parity of standards.

3 Presentation to the customer

The main difference between competing manufacturers, suppliers of services, supermarket chains and multiple stores is in the way they communicate with their customers. It is in this area where the greatest control and direct influence can be brought to bear. In the presentation and pricing of products; in the services and ideas offered to the customer or consumer by means of public relations, advertising and publicity, direct mail, telephone selling, exhibitions and the sales force.

However good all the other methods of persuasive communication are, in the majority of companies the bulk of the presentational effort and persuasion is carried out by the sales force. Their importance can be judged by the fact that in some markets the only difference between competing companies is the relative quality of their sales forces. In markets such as agricultural implements and construction machinery, banking and life assurance, office equipment, the buyer's decision is more often than not determined by who calls on him, what is said to him and how it is said. Now more than ever, a salesman's *authority* and *ability* to *make* and *take* negotiating decisions without reference back to his supervisors is increasingly evident. In many markets, a company relies on its sales force to gain advantage over competitors.

Ironically, the grouping of larger companies into competition with one another, the ease of imitation despite patent laws, the very success of companies to sell their products and services through the efforts of their sales forces, has resulted in other developments which are changing the attitude and role of buyers of products and thus the nature of the selling job.

The changing nature of the selling job

Four major changes are affecting the role and the importance of the sales force.

1 *The growth of multinational companies*

Since 1970 the development of multinational companies whose operations span the globe has accelerated. The products of American, British, Dutch, French, German, Japanese, Swiss, and other international companies, are manufactured in nearly every major country by their own factories or under licence. The European Economic Community has already changed the approach of many capital-goods producers, chemical manufacturers, tyre and rubber combines, retail stores, towards their markets.

2 *Companies are tending to become larger in size but fewer in number*

Takeovers and mergers bear ample and almost daily testimony to this development, frequently encouraged by governments. Before 1939 there were over forty motor-car manufacturers in the United Kingdom. Today there are only four major ones and even the future of some of these cannot be predicted.

In brewing, in food manufacturing, in oil and petroleum, sugar refinery, supermarketing, companies are tending to become larger in size but fewer in number. Such a development means that no supplying company and, in particular, no salesman can hope to retain the business of giant organisations unless product quality and service is sustained.

5

For the salesman and saleswoman whose job it is to develop and maintain business with such giant organisations, the implications are stark. 'I was just passing by so I thought I would pop in to see if there was any business' is thankfully rarely heard by customers when salesmen call on them. No less dangerous is the attitude of any salesman to a call that failed in its objective, either through lack of planning, seeing the wrong buyer, discussing the wrong product to meet a particular customer requirement, or failing to understand the customers' profit or cost problems: 'Oh well you can't win them all. I will get the order next time round'. There will not be a next time round for the salesman who has not done his homework before he calls on a customer.

This is true of more and more marketing situations. For example, two independent breweries were both taken over by a major hotel group. Before that takeover there were three independent groups of buyers upon whom the salesman of products and services could call and sell, ranging from the supply of bottles, caps, hotel cutlery and crockery, food, industrial cleaning machines, bulk tankers, etc. Now there is either one buyer or one buying committee. This committee will not convene nor give a second interview to any salesman who has neither studied their needs nor developed relevant plans and solutions to meet and satisfy them in terms of improving profit opportunities, reducing costs, product quality, pricing and follow-up service and technical advice.

Manufacturing companies also have to market and to advertise their products to help sell them and so need effective creative and, above all, efficient advertising agents to help them invest their money on promotion wisely.

Advertising agencies have experienced a marked decline in profit margins and so every account must be profitable. If, due to mistakes, an advertising agency has to spend more time on an account worth, say, £100,000 a year, it could cost them more money to service it than it is worth.

3 Buyers are becoming increasingly powerful

Because of the concentration of strength, buyers in larger companies, manufacturers and retail distribution chains of products, services or ideas, whose purchases represent a major percentage of the supplying company's turnover and profits, are becoming much more powerful. Each purchasing decision they make, the size of the orders they can give, the effect they can have upon the subsequent purchases of products, can have dramatic repercussions upon every facet of the supplying business, from cash flow, production, distribution, and finally even to the levels of employment, as the stock control decisions made by Marks & Spencer demonstrated throughout 1975 upon some of their suppliers such as Corahs.

Matching this increased power and influence, these buyers are becoming much more knowledgeable and well informed about the *products and manufacturing processes of their suppliers*; in *finance* and the financial effects on profitability of their buying decisions, particularly when they buy to re-sell; in *negotiating* the purchase of supplies, and above all in their own *marketing* and *selling*.

An electronics group, employing over seventy thousand people, one of the world's largest car manufacturers and a Swiss chemical group have taken the education and skills development of their purchasing officers to the point where they are not only trained to buy but are given selling courses alongside their own company's sales force so that they have a better understanding of the selling techniques used by salesmen who call on them.

4 Competition

Competition between these giant organisations is increasing to the point that, not only are they employing many more methods of presentation and communication (including telephone selling), but they are taking over their distributors or, alternatively, developing their own powerful distribution outlets so that they can control the factors that influence buyers' decisions. For example, tyre manufacturers have taken over their tyre distribution networks; agricultural feed and fertiliser manufacturers have taken over not only agricultural merchants but some of their larger consumers of animal feeds, such as egg producers. A paint, wallpaper and textile fabrics group is setting up a national chain of home decorating and furnishing shops, to cater for the housewife who wants to have advice on how to blend all factors together to make her home attractive and to make her purchases at one place instead of going to a number of different shops; a glass tableware manufacturer now not only sells their own manufactured products to hotels and restaurants, but also all the other items that are needed, such as cutlery, table linen, table mats, etc.

The changing role of the sales force

The role and importance of the sales force is not lessened by factors of economic life and changes occurring in the market places in which a company operates. Far from it. The sales force will have a more decisive influence upon the success of marketing strategies and plans as their work becomes more specific. Companies have come to recognise that customers create a business; only by keeping them satisfied and by meeting their requirements can a company survive and prosper. If they don't others will.

This means that in order to deal with and take commercial advantage of these changes, companies have continually to improve their methods of marketing and selling, above all to ensure that the sales force is *organised* to deal with these larger *key* buyers and has the relevant new knowledge and skills to plan and achieve *profitable* business with major market segments and key individual customers.

Customers are becoming more knowledgeable, not only about the products and services they buy or reject but *how to buy them*, and so they are far more critical of those who supply them. The salesmen who sell to them must be more professional. Whilst all commercial organisations seek a financial objective, the margins of error are now so narrow that salesmen will be needed as never before to perform a vital but changing function. Where once the results of selling were measured and rewarded in terms of the volume, units or tonnages, increasingly they are being judged by the amount of profit produced. Where once the salesman was a jack of all trades, selling everything to every outlet or customer, he must now specialise in directing his selling skills to carefully selected markets and to key buyers. The sales force and each member of it must be the spearhead and apex of a triangle through which more costly and tailored company resources will flow.

New skills needed

All these factors are going to make selling a much more creative job, providing opportunities for a new and more influential role in the company, based upon three key skills:

1   Knowledge of the financial and operational needs of his own company and of the customer's business and how to apply that knowledge in his selling to major customers.
2   Knowledge and ability to plan long term mutually profitable customer strategies and to implement those strategies and plans successfully.
3   Knowledge, skill and expertise to negotiate profitable business with key accounts.

The principles, knowledge, methods and techniques salesmen and saleswomen can use to develop their skills and expertise in these three key areas, *finance*, *planning* and *sales negotiation*, are set out in the following chapters.

2 Improving business performance

In running a business both buyer and seller are subject to the same commercial realities and disciplines. Profit is the ultimate objective, although there may be many other goals which individual companies seek to achieve. But profit, how much is made and over what period, is the yardstick by which commercial and industrial companies are judged by those who own them – the shareholders. 'PROFIT', as William Howlett of Consolidated Foods Corporation aptly put it in 1966, stands for: 'Proper Return on Funds Invested Today and Tomorrow'. Buyers are buying profit opportunities, whilst those who sell to them do so in order to make a profit.

But until recently salesmen have not been deeply involved in or even aware of – assuming that their companies or customers allow them to be – the overall effect of their products and services upon the profitability of a customer's business. Today the need to understand the principles of finance and how to apply and use them in selling is essential for a number of reasons:

1 Customers buy products as a part of their management task of helping them to achieve their profit objectives. Buyers are becoming more efficient in running their companies and more astute in their buying as competition for their business and competition in the markets to which they sell increase.

2 As companies, through takeovers and mergers, grow larger in size but fewer in number, so the orders that are placed become larger but the buying points are becoming fewer in most industries.

3 Because of the speed with which even newly launched and successful products can be copied, resulting in profit opportunities being slashed overnight by competition, companies have had to become expert in financial controls and management accounting.

4 For this reason, buyers need far more objective proof of financial gain from their major buying decisions from those who sell to them.

5 The application of financial techniques in marketing and the routine use of common standards and controls by which

companies can measure their performance week by week, month by month and year by year.

6 The increasingly complex decisions customers have to make about products and their relative value and benefits when so often superficially they look alike.

A sound knowledge of finance applied to selling will enable you to understand the changing needs of your customers' business and thus put you in a much better position to help make the best possible contribution to achieving both volume and profit goals for your key customers and for your own company.

Finance affects everyone in a business and should therefore be understood by everyone and not left solely to accountants. Too often in recent years non-financial people, particularly in marketing and in selling, have regarded finance as a mystical subject. In reality, as you shall see, it is relatively easy to acquire a practical and working knowledge and develop it as a selling skill on the job.

There are three main aspects of finance that you need to grasp:

1 The operation of finance in a business.
2 The measurement of business performance in financial terms.
3 The role of the sales force in achieving business results expressed in financial terms.

Let us examine these three aspects in detail and, through simple examples, familiarise ourselves with how money works.

The operation of finance in a business

All businesses, from the corner shop to the vast industrial corporations, supermarketing chains and financial institutions are governed by their ability to attract and use money and people to make profits.

The ingredients of commercial success thus depend upon the ability of the management of a business to use the resources they have obtained with the money they have attracted in the most effective and efficient way. This can be in one or a combination of methods, for example by:

1 Making more sales.
2 Increasing the margin between costs and selling prices.
3 Increasing output in relation to costs (remember how, to their surprise, many British companies during the three-day week in

the winter of 1973 produced as much as during a normal five-day working week).

4   Using less money to run the business (reducing the amount of reserve stocks and the amount of interest paid on money borrowed from the bank to finance such stocks).

5   Reducing production costs by replacing old, slow-working machinery by new plant able to produce twice as much in the same time as the old, etc.

So money provides the wherewithal to obtain the resources of people, machinery, raw materials and all the other requirements upon which profits are based. But it is not just creating resources that builds a business. The lubricant that makes a business run smoothly and profitably is the *flow of funds*. The salesman needs to understand the source of this flow, the nature and kinds of business activities which influence it and how the behaviour of these funds are recorded on paper.

Indeed it is by understanding such records and what they tell him that the salesman can make any plans to contribute to a customer's profit improvement. Figure 2.1 illustrates, in very simple terms, the business process of attracting and using resources to generate profits.

Recording business performance

Money invested in a business exists in many forms: as plant and machinery; as raw materials; as work-in-progress and finished goods in warehouses; as goods and services sold to customers but not yet paid for.

In order to measure how successful the management of a business is in making the most effective use of these resources, it is essential to be able to record in commonly understood financial terms how a company is performing. The success or otherwise of management performance is usually expressed by means of financial accounts, of which the two most important are: the balance sheet and the profit and loss account. The law requires all limited companies to publish these accounts in a prescribed form at least annually. By this means the proprietors of the company can see how their funds have been used and the profits (or losses) that have been made, and the company's creditors or intending creditors can judge the soundness of the business. What do these two financial statements tell you about a company?

1   *A balance sheet* is a statement showing the financial position of a company at a specific date. It summarises what a company *owns* (its *assets*) and what it *owes* (its *liabilities*). See Figure 2.2.

11

2   *A profit and loss account* is a statement of a company's trading
      performance, *over a stated period of time*, showing how
      revenues were made, the costs incurred, and finally the profit
      made. See Figure 2.5.

Comparing these two statutory documents, the profit and loss account
gives you a picture, in monetary terms, of the buying, making and selling
of a company's products *over a period* (usually twelve months); the
balance sheet is a still-life picture, in monetary terms, summarising what
the position was on the last day of that twelve-month period in terms of
the sources of money and how it has been used.

Now let us examine these two documents in more detail so that you
understand the principles upon which they are constructed, their form
and content.

Balance sheet

A balance sheet is designed to communicate two pieces of information:
what a particular company *owns* at a stated date; and what that
company *owes* at a stated date.

Assets

The assets in a balance sheet are what a company owns. If necessary they
can all *in time* be converted into cash, but those which can readily and
quickly be realised are known as *current assets*, whilst those unlikely to
be converted are known as *fixed assets*.

Fixed assets consist of items likely to be used over a longer period of
time than one year by a company and may include:

    (a) land;
    (b) buildings;
    (c) plant and machinery;
    (d) transport;
    (e) furniture and fixtures, etc.

Current assets consist of items for short term use during the operating
twelve months' cycle of a company and may include:

    (a) raw materials;
    (b) stocks;

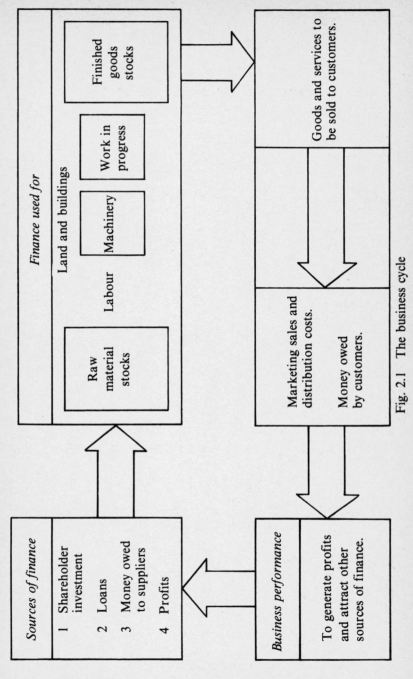

Fig. 2.1 The business cycle

(c) work in progress;
(d) finished stocks;
(e) debtors (money owed by customers who have bought goods but not yet paid for them);
(f) cash, etc.

Liabilities

The balancing factor in a balance sheet is the liabilities which represent what a company *owes*. Liabilities may be divided into three groups:

Shareholders' funds for the company's long-term use are not normally liable to be repaid quickly. They include:

(a) share capital (the money put into a business by the owners);
(b) capital surplus (profits realised from the sale of assets);
(c) reserves (accumulated profit available for distribution but retained as provision against unforeseen possibilities).

Long-term liabilities for the company's long-term use are not normally liable to be repaid quickly. They include:

(a) long-term bank loans;
(b) mortgages;
(c) bonds, etc.

Current liabilities. These consist of monies owed and likely to be due for payment within the company's current operating business cycle (normally twelve months or less). They include:

(a) creditors (money owed to other people);
(b) bank overdraft;
(c) taxes;
(d) dividends to shareholders;
(e) interest due on loans.

Why is a balance sheet so called?

Traditionally, balance sheets have been drawn up showing the total liabilities on the left-hand side and the total assets on the right-hand side. When the values given to each section on either side are added up they must balance. How does this happen? Money subscribed by shareholders to start a company is used to buy assets, such as buildings, plant machinery, raw materials, and all the other necessities to enable

FARR & WYDE LIMITED
Balance sheet, 31 March 1977

	£		£
Share capital		Fixed assets	
100,000 Ordinary shares	100,000	Freehold property	50,000
		Fixtures and equipment	
		at cost *less* depreciation	30,000
Reserves			80,000
Profit and loss account			
(unappropriated balance)	20,000		
Shareholders' funds	120,000		
		Current assets	
Long-term liabilities		Stock	40,000
Loans	20,000	Debtors	35,000
		Cash	15,000
Current liabilities			90,000
Corporation tax	7,000		
Creditors	18,000		
Ordinary dividend	5,000		
	30,000		
	£170,000		£170,000

Figure 2.2   Balance sheet

products or services to be produced. So £100,000 of shareholders' funds
– a liability in a company balance sheet – is balanced by the value of the
assets that money or a proportion of it is used to purchase. This is shown
in the specimen balance sheet in Figure 2.2.

A balance sheet will normally show not only the financial position of a
company at a particular date, but also the figures for the previous year
or period, thus providing a comparison.

You can also assess the *solvency* and *liquidity* of a company from the
figures presented in a balance sheet. Solvency is the ability to meet
outside liabilities from total assets. Liquidity is a company's ability to
meet its current liabilities (pay its creditors, bank interest, etc., on due
dates) from its current assets – notably from cash.

Presentation of accounts

The traditional 'account' format for balance sheets, as shown in Figure
2.3, has now almost universally given way to the 'net asset' format which
highlights capital employed and working capital, as in Figure 2.4. This
narrative form of presentation is laid out as a businessman thinks when
analysing the costs of setting up and running a business.

Liabilities (sources of funds)		Assets (uses of funds)	
	£		£
Share capital and reserves	120,000	Fixed assets	80,000
Long-term liabilities	20,000	Current assets	90,000
Current liabilities	30,000		
	£170,000		£170,000

Figure 2.3   Balance sheet (summary): 'account' format

		£
Share capital and reserves		120,000
Long-term liabilities		20,000
Capital employed		£140,000
Fixed assets		80,000
Current assets	90,000	
Less: Current liabilities	30,000	
Net current assets ('working capital')		60,000
Net assets		£140,000

Figure 2.4   Balance sheet (summary): 'net asset' format

Limitations of the balance sheet

The picture given by the balance sheet of a company is an incomplete one for a number of reasons:

1 It cannot show the market or competitive situations in which a company traded to produce the results.
2 The figures shown cannot in all cases be exact or accurate. The valuation of stock is just one example. Decisions on value which are either very conservative or very optimistic can markedly influence the apparent strength of a company's position.
3 The ability of a company's management team cannot figure, yet it may be a company's major asset.
4 It can only concern itself with those factors which can be expressed in monetary terms.

Profit and loss account

The profit and loss account will show the results of a company's trading performance over the period stated in the document – usually twelve months. It will indicate revenue, costs and profits. See Figure 2.5.

FARR & WYDE LIMITED
Profit and loss account
for the year ending 31 March 1977

	£
Sales	240,000
Trading profit for the year	17,000
Less: Debenture interest	1,000
Profit before tax	16,000
Corporation tax	7,000
Net profit for the year after tax	9,000
Less: Ordinary dividend	5,000
Retained out of the year's profit	4,000
Add: Unappropriated balance brought forward	16,000
Unappropriated balance carried forward	£20,000

Figure 2.5   Profit and loss account

The items identified will vary in type and detail, but normally a profit and loss account has three separate parts:

Trading account, showing:

    (a) sales revenue;
    (b) cost of sales;
    (c) trading profit (or loss).

Profit and loss account, showing:

    (a) trading profit (or loss);
    (b) other income (e.g. interest received);
    (c) expenses (e.g. depreciation, interest paid, directors' fees, auditors' fees, bank and legal charges);
    (d) taxes payable;
    (e) net profit before tax for the year.

Appropriation account, showing how the profit has been 'distributed', e.g. paid as dividends to shareholders, transferred to reserves, accumulated as unappropriated profits carried forward to the balance sheet.

The profit and loss account provides a detailed picture of how well or badly a company is trading and how profitable or otherwise the various sections of the business are. As a salesman you have a major influence on the figures that appear in the trading account section, in terms of sales revenue and the costs of sales, e.g. sales revenue results from:

    (a) number of units/services sold;
    (b) prices obtained;
    (c) mix of sales.

Cost of sales include:

    (a) selling costs;
    (b) marketing costs;
    (c) administrative costs;
    (d) distribution costs;
    (e) production costs.

But in order to draw conclusions from such financial statements necessary to understand the relationships between a number of item which are in different forms, such as:

(a) the capital originally invested in a business;
(b) the plant and machinery and the extent to which it is fully utilised in producing finished products;
(c) the relationship between sales being made and availability of finished stocks;
(d) the balance between sales being made and money owed to customers, etc.

All these business relationships help to make up a picture of a company's business performance. These relationships between various activities and the financial results they produce in the balance sheet and profit and loss account are of the utmost importance in understanding *why* a business is doing well or badly and above all *where* adjustments or corrections need to be made.

Measuring business performance

The successful business managers you sell to and negotiate with measure and assess their purchasing, trading and financial operations on a continuous basis. This enables them to take advantage of favourable marketing conditions or avoid risks, such as building up stocks of raw materials when prices are rising or having to borrow money at high rates of interest to keep customers supplied because credit control is out of hand and customers are delaying paying their accounts.

By looking at the relationships between key factors in a business, management can assess not only the effects of those decisions and business activities but also the causes.

The figures in a company's accounts can be made much more understandable if they are related to each other in a series of ratios. Such ratios can then be used to analyse past performance and to plan future performance. (See Table 2.1 key profitability ratios.)

The most widely used *overall* measurement of performance is the amount of profit made in relation to the capital employed in a business. Capital employed is a company's total assets minus its current liabilities. Profitability is usually expressed in the financial ratios we will now examine as the Return (R) on Capital employed (CE). So the primary

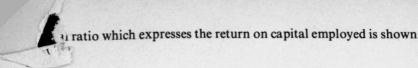

...ratio which expresses the return on capital employed is shown

$$\frac{\text{Return}}{\text{Capital employed}} \quad \text{or} \quad \frac{\text{R}}{\text{CE}}$$

It is the financial expression of the effectiveness of a company's management and can be used to compare one business with another or to other alternative forms of investment. It makes us ask the question: 'Would we have done better to use our money in some other way?'

The Return on Capital employed in a business results from two other financial measurements. They are:

Return on Sales, which is the net profit before tax expressed as a percentage of sales and shown as:

$$\frac{\text{Return}}{\text{Sales}} \quad \text{or} \quad \frac{\text{R}}{\text{S}}$$

Sales on Capital employed, which is the number of times capital is turned over in relation to sales made and is shown as

$$\frac{\text{Sales}}{\text{Capital employed}} \quad \text{or} \quad \frac{\text{S}}{\text{CE}}$$

These three key ratios can be combined to present a financial picture of actual or planned performance.

Figure 2.6 illustrates a 'hierarchy' of management ratios used by operating managers in a business to analyse profitability. It is called a 'hierarchy' because at one end can be seen how these ratios influence the total profit of a business, and at the other end how they can be related to individual performance.

Figure 2.7 shows a hierarchy of management ratios in a company that markets warehousing and national distribution services to manufacturing companies producing dry goods.

Table 2.1
Key profitability ratios

Ratio	How to calculate	What it means
1. Return on Capital employed $\dfrac{R}{CE}$ Example: What is the $\dfrac{R}{CE}$ of Farr & Wyde Limited?	$\dfrac{\text{Net profit before tax}}{\text{Total assets employed minus current liabilities}}\%$ $\dfrac{16,000}{(170,000-30,000)\ 140,000} = 12\%*$	It measures the effectiveness of management. It measures the earning of a sufficient return on investment in assets to ensure perpetuation of investment/profit/investment cycle.
2. Return on sales $\dfrac{R}{S}$ Example: What is the $\dfrac{R}{S}$ of Farr & Wyde Limited?	$\dfrac{\text{Net profit before tax}}{\text{Net sales}}\%$ $\dfrac{16,000}{240,000} = 7\%*$	Measures the success any company has achieved in meeting the objective of realising profit from each pound's worth of products or services it sells.
3. Turnover of Capital employed $\dfrac{S}{CE}$ Example: What is the $\dfrac{S}{CE}$ of Farr & Wyde Limited?	$\dfrac{\text{Sales}}{\text{Total assets minus current liabilities}}$ $\dfrac{240,000}{(170,000-30,000)\ 140,000} = 1.7*$	This ratio also measures the effectiveness of management – whether it is doing an adequate job with regard to sales in relation to assets employed.

*Figures rounded for simplicity

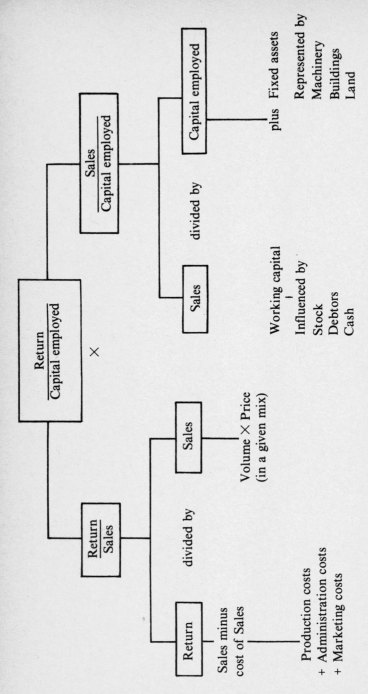

Figure 2.6   Return on capital employed formula

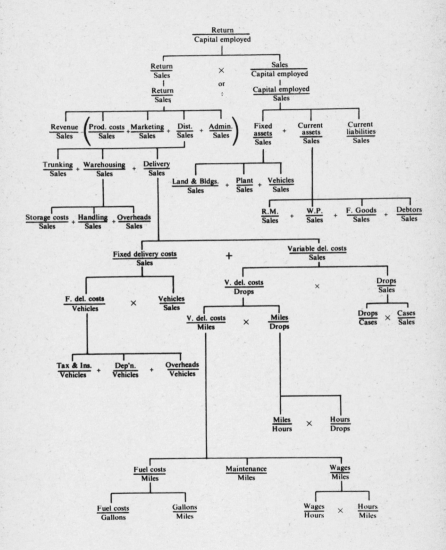

Figure 2.7 Return on capital employed formula for a national warehousing and distribution company

The number and type of ratios used and their relative importance is individual to every business. The interpretation of the ratios is also individual to every business. Here is a comparison made possible by using the financial ratios of two widely differing business enterprises:

A distributive business

Fixed capital is low in relation to working capital employed.

Therefore Sales : Capital employed – the number of times capital is turned over – is crucial.

Low ratio of return on sales but rapid turnover produces ROCE objective:

$$\frac{R}{S} = 4\%$$

ROCE 24%

$$\frac{S}{CE} = 6\times$$

Therefore key management activity:

(a) achieve rapid stock turn;
(b) fine control of buying and selling prices;
(c) make optimum use of warehouse space and transport.

A heavy engineering business

Margin on sales is much more important. The high proportion of fixed capital employed in the business means capital turnover is inevitably slower:

$$\frac{R}{S} = 12\%$$

ROCE 24%

$$\frac{S}{CE} = 2.0\times$$

Therefore key management activity:

(a) control manufacturing costs;
(b) maintain output;
(c) control capital employed;
(d) maintain margins.

Now the figures from these same two businesses, and those already given for Farr & Wyde Limited, are brought together to show how different types of business can achieve the same return on capital employed from very different return on sales (i.e. margins) and sales on capital employed. The influences of the sales force are listed.

$\dfrac{\text{Return}}{\text{Capital employed}}$	equals $=$	$\dfrac{\text{Return}}{\text{Sales}}$	multiplied by $\times$	$\dfrac{\text{Sales}}{\text{Capital employed}}$
Engineering	12% =	8%	×	1.5
Consumer	12% =	4%	×	3
Farr & Wyde Limited	12% =	7%	×	1.7

<table>
<tr><td>Influenced by:</td><td>Influenced by:</td></tr>
<tr><td>(a) volume;</td><td>(a) volume;</td></tr>
<tr><td>(b) price;</td><td>(b) price;</td></tr>
<tr><td>(c) costs;</td><td>(c) stock control;</td></tr>
<tr><td>(d) mix of products sold.</td><td>(d) control of debtors;</td></tr>
<tr><td></td><td>(e) use of fixed assets.</td></tr>
</table>

These financial ratios can be broken down further to reveal other important ratios which measure business performance, e.g.

1   Is profitability falling: $\dfrac{\text{Return}}{\text{Capital employed}}$?

2   To what is this due: $\dfrac{\text{Return}}{\text{Sales}}$ or $\dfrac{\text{Sales}}{\text{Capital employed}}$?

3   If it is $\dfrac{\text{Return}}{\text{Sales}}$ what changes have occurred?

4   How can we identify these changes:

(a) price changes?
(b) product mix changes?
(c) cost changes?
(d) volume changes?

5   If falling profitability is due to $\dfrac{\text{Sales}}{\text{Capital employed}}$

is this due to $\dfrac{\text{Sales}}{\text{Fixed assets}}$ or $\dfrac{\text{Sales}}{\text{Working capital}}$?

6   If due to $\dfrac{\text{Sales}}{\text{Fixed assets}}$ is this *either* under-utilisation of plant and machinery *or* because new assets are not yet producing a return?

25

7   If due to $\dfrac{\text{Sales}}{\text{Working capital}}$ is this:

     either a stock turnover problem: $\dfrac{\text{Stock} \times 365 \text{ days}}{\text{Sales revenue}}$

     or a debtor turnover problem: $\dfrac{\text{Debtors} \times 365 \text{ days}}{\text{Sales revenue}}$

Ratios can be extended to the point where perhaps a works manager looks at the output per hour on his machines, or a transport manager examines cost per mile or delivery cost per pack. Meanwhile, your customers are analysing profit on capital turnover in relation to feet of facings, or the cost of assembly per order. See Table 2.1.

The financial effects of the sales negotiator

The key account negotiator can have a major impact on his company's profitability through the effective use of his selling and negotiating skills influenced by such financial ratios as those illustrated in the distributive and heavy engineering examples on page 24.

You can 'read' your effect on your business by examining the two ratios:

$$\frac{\text{Return}}{\text{Sales}} \quad \text{and} \quad \frac{\text{Sales}}{\text{Capital employed}}$$

Whilst as salesmen you probably do not set the standards in these areas of financial performance, it is nevertheless your responsibility to achieve them because the standards set in each of these areas add up to the returns from the sales target set for the company in relation to the amount of capital we tie up in doing it.

Cash flow

Sales and marketing people are most often concerned with sales volume and turnover, not with the actual receipt and payment of cash. As soon as an order is taken, the sale for the salesman is complete. *When* the money is paid is generally outside his control.

However, for the company the important measure is *cash flow*, i.e. the flow of funds in and out of the company. Only cash pays bills, and lack of it even for a short period is a common cause of bankruptcy. Cash-flow forecasting is essential for management to plan its use of resources and to recognise cash needs in the future. Cash flow is forecast by:

1 Producing a detailed sales forecast, related to cash generated.
2 Relating cost of sales to cash outgoings.
3 Including all capital expenditure when it occurs.
4 Establishing cash requirements for the business.

The main points for sales and marketing people to note about cash flow are:

1 The importance of accurate sales forecasting.
2 The need to speed up payment of invoices.
3 The need to hold low stocks relative to sales volume.
4 The drain on cash caused by sudden sales volume increases (because the goods or component materials have to be paid for before sales revenue is received).
5 The need to improve sales margins.
6 The need to curb interest costs incurred by funding rapid sales increases, or sales shortfalls on budget.

The following example illustrates how profit shown on a profit and loss account bears no relation to cash actually generated and used by the business.

Cash budgeting

Problem

Company A manufactures and sells a product which retails for £1,000. Manufacturing costs are £500 per unit, other costs total £10,000 per month. The company gets paid on average one month after invoicing, invoices being sent when the product is dispatched; raw materials and labour costs are incurred on average one month before sale. There is a seasonal sales pattern which rises during the first half of the year to a summer peak, falling during the second half to the lowest figure in December and January.

The company's cash situation is tight and therefore the managing director has asked the sales manager to prepare a forecast for the first six months of next year. This is:

> *Revenue, Cost and Profit forecast*
> *6 months January–June inclusive*
> *Revenue* 210 units at £1,000   £210,000
> *Cost* Manufacturing costs 210 at £500   £105,000
> Other costs at £10,000 per month   £60,000   £165,000
>
>   Profit   £45,000

The managing director is very pleased with this but decides to analyse it in a little more detail to see the cash-flow situation.

Assumptions

1   Assume sales pattern:

D	J	F	M	A	M	J	J
10	10	20	30	40	50	60	60

2   Assume no cash brought forward at beginning of period. See page 29.

Some key financial terms

Return: Net profit (usually before tax and sometimes before interest charges where levied by a parent company or a subsidiary).

Capital employed: Fixed assets plus working capital.

Fixed assets: Money tied up in land, buildings, plant and machinery, etc.

Current assets: Money tied up in stock, work in progress, debtors, cash, etc.

Current liabilities: Money owed in the short term, e.g. creditors, overdraft, tax, dividends.

Working capital: Current assets minus current liabilities.

Fixed liabilities: The long term money in the company, i.e. shareholders, equity, long-term loans, retained profits.

Margin: Sales revenue minus cost of goods sold.

Balance sheet: Statement of a company's position at one moment in time, usually at the end of the financial year, showing the sources of the money in the company (fixed liabilities plus current liabilities) and how it is deployed (fixed assets plus current assets).

Profit and loss account: Statement showing the results of a company trading in the period indicating revenue, expenditure, and thus profit.

Answer to problem

	D	J	F	M	A	M	J	J
Sales forecast	10	10	20	30	40	50	60	60
Revenue		10,000	10,000	20,000	30,000	40,000	50,000	
Manufacturing costs		10,000	15,000	20,000	25,000	30,000	30,000	
Other costs		10,000	10,000	10,000	10,000	10,000	10,000	
Total costs		20,000	25,000	30,000	35,000	40,000	40,000	
Surplus		-10,000	-15,000	-10,000	- 5,000	-	+10,000	
Brought forward		-	-10,000	-25,000	-35,000	40,000	-40,000	
Carried forward		-10,000	-25,000	-35,000	-40,000	-40,000	-30,000	

3 Improving customers' profits

The skilled application of financial knowledge gives you a very powerful tool which can be used to influence the profitability not only of your own but also your customer's business. By analysing the customer's business needs in financial terms you can develop and present benefits in financial terms.

Analysing customers' accounts

A close examination of the Return on sales and the Sales on the capital employed will identify opportunities to make the customer's operations more profitable.

Return on sales

This figure is the result of sales revenue minus the cost of generating it. You may be able to improve it by reducing the customer's costs in certain areas, for example:

Operational costs. Can you offer:

    (a) better delivery arrangements?
    (b) easier, more economic processes?
    (c) less damage or waste?
    (d) easier handling?
    (e) more economic use of labour or raw materials?
    (f) more economic use of space?

Sales and distribution costs. Can you offer:

    (a) more economic selling methods? (through sales aids);
    (b) better use of salesmen's time? (through stimulation of demand);
    (c) lower transport costs?
    (d) fewer complaints?

Administration costs. Can you offer:

    (a) streamlined paper work systems?
    (b) less time spent on administration?
    (c) fewer administrative tasks?
    (d) better payment terms?
    (e) simpler stock control and order system?

Alternatively, you may not be able to reduce his costs but you can increase his Return on sales by helping him to:

    (a) achieve a higher margin;
    (b) get a better product mix;
    (c) sell more effectively;
    (d) increase his sale of complementary lines.

Sales to capital employed

This figure represents the volume or value of sales compared with assets required to generate it. You may be able to improve this figure either by helping the customer increase the volume or value of his sales, or by reducing the value of assets involved.

Sales volume or value. Can you offer:

    (a) greater acceptance of your products by his markets?
    (b) greater market penetration for his products or services?
    (c) help with advertising, selling, etc?
    (d) better sales results from salesmen, transport, etc?
    (e) more effective promotions?
    (f) merchandising support?
    (g) reduced out-of-stock?

Asset reduction. Can you offer:

    (a) less capital tied up in stocks?
    (b) less space required to stock?
    (c) faster through-put?
    (d) fewer debtors?
    (e) better use of spare cash?
    (f) better use of existing fitments and space?

An example

Consider the following key ratios taken from the annual accounts of two comparable grocery firms:

	Superstores		Prestwicks	
	1976	1975	1976	1975
Return on capital employed	26.2%	35.9%	30.7%	35.0%
Return on sales	4.6%	5.8%	2.0%	2.1%
Sales to capital employed	5.6%	6.2%	15.2%	16.6%
Sales to fixed assets	6.6%	6.3%	14.1%	10.9%
Sales to working capital	36.0%	67.8%	–	–
Stock turnover	42 days	41 days	24 days	27 days
Debtor turnover	3 days	4 days	–	–
Creditor turnover	43 days	48 days	26 days	31 days

The main points to note are:

1 The very high Return on capital employed of Prestwicks, made up of a low margin but very high asset turnover.
2 The decline in profit margins on sales, a result of cost inflation and government controls.
3 The dependence of wholesalers and retailers on credit from manufacturers to fund the business. Prestwicks has, in fact, a *negative* working capital, i.e. current liabilities exceed current assets.
4 The improved Stock turnover of Prestwicks, which leads to a higher asset/turnover ratio.

The implications of this analysis for negotiations are:

1 Retailers and wholesalers need a very high return from any capital invested. Can your ideas help?
2 Retailers and wholesalers are under pressure on margins on sales, which implies more pressure on terms from suppliers, especially overriders.
3 Retailers will be very interested in a higher rate of stock-turn to improve the Sales to capital employed ratio when sales margins

are falling. Can you demonstrate this in negotiations? (*Note:* Superstores' slower rate of Stock turnover is caused mainly by non-food sales.)

In practice, you will be able to obtain much more information on your accounts' business than that contained in annual reports, e.g. gross margins, stock turnover by line, cash margins. Use of this data can form the basis of very effective negotiations by showing how well you understand the customer, his problems and his objectives.

Analysing customer business needs

You can look at the use of financial knowledge in analysing customer business needs by considering some further examples:

1 Selling to multiple grocery outlets

This requires skilled negotiation. The major national outlets have prospered through their ability to manage financial resources in large-scale distribution.

The salesman in this situation needs to discuss not only his product and its appeal to the housewife, but also its potential profitability to the distributor, not just its profitability per unit, but its profitability in terms of turnover of stock relative to the volume and location of the space occupied in comparison with a vast range of alternatives open to the store.

The salesman must therefore be able to discuss, for example, with the buyer:

1   The sales of his product per foot of space occupied.
2   The stock-turn ratio – how many times the stock will turnover and make use of the space allocated to it.
3   The margin per unit × stock-turn to give margin per foot of space.
4   The relationship between promotional costs, discounts, volume, stock-turn and margin.
5   The relationship between site in store and the achievement of target sales and margins.

2 Selling to the agricultural industry

This is one of the most competitive for any salesman. Many of the products sold to agriculture have become commodities as technical differences have narrowed or disappeared.

Some of the most successful agricultural salesmen succeed in this situation by selling from a financial base. They sell not products, but management systems which enable the customer to make most profitable use of the product. The salesman is trained to discuss and analyse business ratios with his customers and to help the customer to improve his business performance.

As just one case, an agricultural salesman selling to a bacon pig production unit is in a much stronger selling position if he can discuss, for example, with his businessman customer:

Costs of production per lb of liveweight gained:

- (a) how his products can reduce that cost;
- (b) the implications in terms of profitability;
- (c) the implications in terms of return on capital invested.

Capital costs related to the efficiency of alternative production systems:

- (a) matching system to capital available;
- (b) sources of finance and supportive enterprise budgets;
- (c) cash-flow implications.

Cost of production to return per unit of sales:

- (a) relationship between cost and return;
- (b) implications of increasing unit costs in return for greater increase in unit returns;
- (c) margin as a percentage of output;
- (d) how his products can improve the ratio.

3   Selling capital equipment and industrial machinery

The salesman can no longer depend on easily identified product advantages to win a sale. He can sell more easily if he is able, for example, to identify:

1   Whether the customer should buy, rent or lease?
2   What form of finance is most appropriate to the customer's business?
3   What capital allowances are available?

4   In what ways do purchase costs, running costs, maintenance costs and output performance affect the profitability to the customer?

The salesman should therefore be able to use 'financial merchandising' techniques. He may therefore need to discuss, for example, with the buyer:

1   The best use of capital in the business, relating availability of capital to the efficiency of the business at present and as projected.
2   The tax implications of purchasing equipment outright, leasing it, or using loading facilities. Sources of finance.
3   The output of equipment relative to its capital costs and running costs. (The most expensive equipment to buy might well produce the most economic output.)
4   The needs of the business in financial terms and how these affect the purchase decision: e.g., the buyer who is purchasing equipment for rehire has different financial needs to the user purchasing for his own use.
5   The cost of equipment relative to savings in labour costs or increase in output.

In all three examples of selling, financial knowledge enables value to be added to the product and is a major aid to making sales.

Developing and presenting financial benefits

Development

You all know that a 'benefit' is what your product or service offers to the buyer, and that the most effective benefits are those which do something for him which he wants done and can recognise. It is one thing to use financial knowledge to identify customer needs – but sales success depends on your skill in developing and presenting financial benefits persuasively.

Financial benefits should be *understandable*, *accurate* and *attractive*, and need careful presentation. In developing them you need to ask:

1   What does the buyer want done? For example:

  (a) savings in costs?
  (b) increase in output?
  (c) improvement in cash flow?
  (d) more efficiency?
  (e) easier administration?
  (f) increase in sales?
  (g) improvement in profit?
  (h) increase in value of his product?
  (i) improved labour relations?
  (j) financial security?
  (k) convenience?

2   What is the value of the benefit to his business – at what cost?
3   What financial and management measurements are key to his business?
4   How do the benefits offered by your product or service affect these measurements?
5   How can these effects be explained and presented attractively in financial terms?

Financial merchandising

Presentation of financial benefits can be described as 'financial merchandising'. Done well it can add value to the offering which is disproportionate to the real value.

For example, one company operating in a high-volume commodity market no longer 'sells' its products to major customers. What it does is to provide a management accounting service to these customers to help them to make the most profitable use of the products in their business. The service is self-help, with some assistance from technical representatives. At relatively low cost the company maintains high-volume customers by helping them to run their businesses more effectively.

A commodity has derived added value from financial merchandising. In more immediate and practical terms, you can produce financial benefits during sales interviews by developing aids designed to link your offering with the customer's business. For example, a company selling process equipment and materials uses the format in Figures 3.1a and 3.1b very effectively to progress from the identification of financial needs to purchase order during the interview.

Prepared for: Name: ....

Title: ....

Company: ....

Location: ....

SAVINGS FOLLOWING INSTALLATION   Annual
                                                                                                   savings

1 *Material savings*   Used/yr   Price

   Present material   .... $\times$ .... = ...
   Proposed material   .... $\times$ .... = ...
   Net savings

2 *Labour savings*
   Machine clean-up ....hrs/yr $\times$ £.............. per hr   =
   Material handling time ....hrs/yr $\times$ £.............. per hr   =
   Reduction in direct labour hours to produce
      same yearly requirements .... $\times$ £............. per hr   =

3 *Increased machine productivity*
   Added capacity
   Reduced floor space..................sq ft $\times$ £.............. per sq ft =
   Elimination of bottlenecks

4 *Reduced rework or scrap*
   Labour savings   ....hrs $\times$ .... per hr
   Savings on packs
   Product saving

5 *Other benefits*
   Eliminated process failures
   Standardised materials
   Other – specify

_____

Total savings..

Total equipment investment...

_____

Figure 3.1a Customer financial needs analysis form

Details of installation: ....

EQUIPMENT REQUIRED

Description	Part no.	Quantity	Price	
			Unit	Total
Pumping unit				
Working heads				
Injectors				
Hoses				
Couplings				
Controls				
Thermostats				
Solenoids				
Solvent fluid				
Oiler				
Oil				
Others				
Total equipment investment				

Signature: .... Title: .... Date: .... 19 ....

Figure 3.1b

The use of financial knowledge as an aid to both buyer and seller

Similar objectives

Buyer and seller work in the same commercial environment. Both buyer and seller are in the long term dependent on achieving similar business objectives.

Balancing the sales and purchase of 'profit'

Whether he is a professional buyer or just a hard-headed businessman, the customer always aims to make the 'best' decision for his business. He tries to balance his use of resources with the objective of maximising his returns, and in doing so must compare what is being offered to him.

The negotiator with financial knowledge benefits in most circumstances

With the professional buyer you can plan your presentation to meet the buyer's needs. You can identify more clearly what those needs are and how your offering can satisfy them. You can talk the same language as the buyer and gain both orders and respect. With the hard-headed businessman you can demonstrate the business advantages being offered. You can identify, with the buyer, business opportunities which the buyer may have overlooked.

Financial knowledge can enable you to:

1 Identify the commercial needs of the business with the buyer.
2 Show how your products or services can meet those needs.
3 Justify and obtain higher prices.
4 Avoid the pitfall of professionally 'selling in' a product which may sell out badly, or prove unsatisfactory in use.
5 Consolidate and obtain more repeat business.
6 Deal better with irrational objections by using demonstrable facts.
7 Predict, show and use post-sale proof of your commercial claims.
8 Be more convincing, confident and authoritative as a negotiator.
9 Identify your sales potential through the eyes of the customer's business.

In exchanging profit opportunities through the proper use of financial knowledge, both buyer and seller benefit, for example:

Benefits to buyer	Benefits to seller
Better and more profitable decisions.	Opportunity to influence those decisions.
Is helped to identify business opportunity.	Trust and repeat business from the buyer.
Looks at all alternatives objectively with you.	You become part of the buyer's business.
Makes the profitable purchases.	Profitable sales.
Is given an objective approach to complex problems.	Convincing sales based on objective information.
Confidence in decisions produces success in use or re-sale.	Success by the buyer produces repeat business.
Greater confidence in supplier and your products or services.	Adds value to the product or service in the face of competition.
Business objectives achieved.	Business objectives achieved.

What do you know? What do you need to know?

Successful business development and negotiation rest upon making products or services that people will need and then being able to *get in* to supply them to the customers you want to supply and *stay in* there. You will have a bank of information about your key customers, which may range from the manufacture of sub-assembly parts for their machines or 'own label' products for them to sell; through what they have purchased from you, how often, what they use your products for, how much they buy from competitors, their financial relationships with you, how often your sales force, or delivery vans, call etc.

The bulk of what you need to know about your key customers' business in order to help improve their profitability you can only find out from your major customers, usually by exploring the following sources of information.

1   *Customers' markets*

   1   What changes are taking place in their markets that are the basis of their demand for your products or services?

2 Will these changes happen overnight or gradually?

3 What new product research, conception, testing or development are they investing in to meet market changes?

4 What information do they collect about the market they serve?

2 Customers' competition

1 Who are their competitors?

2 How strong are they?

3 What share of the markets do they have?

4 If competitors take business from your key customers what will that do to your business overall?

3 The economy of the country

1 Are your key customers likely to be affected by current economic changes?

2 Favourably or unfavourably?

3 If the economy improves, what pressures will this put on your key customers?

4 If it deteriorates how soon will your key customers be affected?

5 What percentage of your key customers' business is done outside the home country? What percentage is home trade?

4 Government legislation

1 What effect will legislation have on your key customers' products, prices, freedom to advertise, profit margins, etc?

2 What effect will foreign government legislation have on your customers' overseas business?

5 New technology

1 How vulnerable are your key customers' products to new developments, new materials?

2 How can your new technology/new developments help them?

3 How soon will new technology threaten your customers' products unless they change?

Conclusion

It has not been the habit of most companies up to now to educate salesmen in areas such as costs, break-even analysis, and the behaviour of markets. But a negotiating salesman must have a working knowledge

Item	Information	Action required

Objectives to be achieved by:

1 Profit improvement objectives
2 Return on capital employed
3 Return on sales
4 Sales revenue
5 Cost reductions

Plans:

1 Profit improvement activities
2 Sales volume projects
3 Market support
4 Cost reduction projects

Timing of activities to achieve objectives

Controls:

1 To measure profit target
2 To measure volume target
3 To measure cost reduction target
4 Contingencies

Figure 3.2 Customer profit plan check-list

of all these and their implications if he is to be able to affect the business of key customers where it matters most – in the amount of profit they make. Only by knowing about these things can he then find answers to the question: What can you do to help me? The answers to that question then enable him to construct a customer plan for the small number of key customer or market segments that contribute the bulk of the profitable sales for which he is held accountable. See Figure 3.2.

4 Costing as an aid to sales

In the development of business with customers a salesman must always keep two considerations in mind when planning the details of his approach and negotiation. First, how to *minimise* the costs customers invest in their products and services upon which their budgeted profits are based. Second, how to *maximise* the profit his company receives from the sales of its products and services. These two objectives are vital in business dealings with the key accounts which contribute the bulk of a company's profits.

To be in a position to influence these two objectives, a salesman must have an accurate and comprehensive knowledge and understanding of costs and profit levels and how these costs and profit levels move in relation to sales volumes produced and to price changes.

The *prices* a company charges for its products or services, the *volume* of sales achieved and the *costs* incurred to produce and sell them are the three key elements which influence profitable marketing. The relationship between *prices*, *volume* and *costs* is not direct and simple, but will conform to certain standards. Prices and sales volume interact with one another to give sales revenue. Obviously the extent to which sales revenue either *exceeds* or falls *below* total costs produces a profit or a loss.

If a salesman is to be in a position to ensure that the products, engineering, processes or services he sells do not result in his customer's costs and therefore market prices being adversely affected, he must understand his customer's markets, pricing and costings.

Definition of costs

In simple terms, the costs a company incurs to develop products or services are of two kinds: *fixed* and *variable*. Fixed costs are sometimes referred to as 'overheads'; and over a defined period, usually of a year or more and within specified ranges or limits, do not vary with changes or variations in volume output. Fixed costs will usually include:

1   Management salaries and related expenses.
2   Rents, rates, heating, lighting, telephone, telex, etc.
3   Office expenses.
4   Fixed costs of sales force salaries, cars, equipment.

Variable costs are those which literally vary according to the volume of products produced or services held available and sold and include:

1   Raw materials and consumable supplies.
2   Direct labour costs.
3   Fuel and power related to specified production processes.
4   Packaging.
5   Commission to agents, distributors, salesmen.
6   Royalties on sales, etc.

The distinction between fixed and variable costs is not absolute and clear-cut and for this reason operating management (and not the accountant) needs to decide how such costs are to be treated. Management approaches the problem of defining what are fixed and what are variable by bearing in mind a number of factors.

If a cost is deemed variable, such as direct labour hired for a specific process, it may need a more complicated and costly control system to measure it so that a true cost is finally reflected in the selling price.

When in doubt in such a situation, optimistic managers will call a cost variable, whereas a pessimist confronted by the same question will call such a cost fixed. What should happen in a well-run business is to analyse the way costs have moved in the past in relation to volume and whether the pattern in the future will continue as before or change and then make a decision which reflects as nearly as possible the truth as it is measured.

Allocation of costs

Having defined costs as either fixed or variable, the next task is to allocate such costs to the various products or services marketed by a company. In the rare event of a company only having one product or service this task is unnecessary! Variable costs are usually not difficult to allocate to individual products. Indeed they may well have been calculated by product originally.

Fixed costs represent more of a problem. Some companies allocate fixed costs in the production area on a physical basis. Rents, rates, lighting, heating, power, are calculated as a cost per square foot. A calculation is then made of the total area taken up by each product, and the costs allocated on this basis. Other fixed costs are allocated on either a value or a unit basis.

Whatever the basis for the allocation of fixed costs to individual products, that allocation can be arbitrary and inaccurate, and give a misleading picture of the true profitability of individual products, and of individual management performance. Indeed, in many companies the allocation of fixed costs is seen to be so inaccurate and time-consuming, that it is not done at all. Instead all fixed costs are put together, and set off against the money that results from sales revenue exceeding variable costs.

The allocation of all costs, both fixed and variable, to individual products is called the *full absorption system*. That is to say, all costs are fully absorbed by all products.

Where only variable costs are allocated to individual products, and fixed costs are expressed as a total, this is called the *contribution system*. That is to say, each product contributes the amount by which its revenue exceeds its variable costs to a pool, out of which fixed costs are paid and net profit before tax remains. The contribution system of cost allocation is now widely accepted as the more realistic system and, importantly, the system which gives the best information on which to base marketing decisions.

Break-even charts

The break-even chart is simply a series of 'photographs' of the business at various levels of activity. It shows the relationship between sales revenue and profits, when profit starts and how it grows. In particular it enables an assessment to be made of risk by illustrating the relationship between the point of break-even and the total projected performance. See Figure 4.1.

Such break-even 'photographs' of various levels of activity and alternatives in a business are not only invaluable internally but, more important, they forewarn the salesman by providing him with an insight into the value or cost impact of a proposition he may put forward to a key account customer and the likely favourable or unfavourable reaction to it.

Examples of the need for advanced knowledge

Let us examine three entirely different commercial situations:

1   A salesman selling a range of chemicals to a company which is considering the possibilities of launching a new product within certain defined cost and price brackets. Unless he can plot the effect on such a customer's fixed and variable costs he cannot even tell whether his price will be acceptable or otherwise.

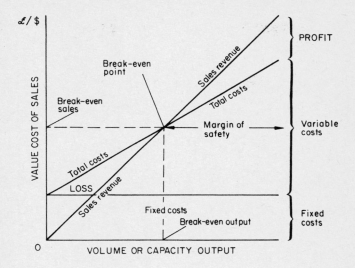

Figure 4.1   Model break-even chart

2   Suppose you are a salesman selling warehousing and distribution services to a food manufacturer. Here again your proposition will stand or fall, not upon the crude price of such a service, but the effect such a service would have upon the food company's existing fixed costs of its present warehousing and the variable costs it incurs in distributing its products to its retail outlets.

3   A salesman selling a service type system – liquid-beverage vending machines on annual rental – to small shops and offices. His proposition may involve a potential customer spending over £1,000 per year to install such a service for his staff of forty people. The price may or may not appear as a major stumbling block. But the chances of his proposition being favourably considered will be greater if he has at his fingertips the knowledge of what costs are incurred by such a company at present to provide liquid refreshment for its staff so that he can compare them with the costs of his proposition and hopefully demonstrate a saving.

How to plot break-even charts

Break-even charts, plotted on graph paper, can provide a salesman with useful information; the management in the company to which he hopes to sell can use this as the basis for making decisions. It is worth the time and effort spent in constructing them. Furthermore, for many people, a graph or picture composed by themselves often enables a situation to be understood much more clearly than a mass of figures.

Let us take four examples, based upon an imaginary company, and working with some simple figures.

Example A

The most simple starting point is to plot a situation where cost and revenue relationships do not change over the period of a total manufacturing project. In Example A (Figure 4.2), predicted sales of 1,000 manufactured units at £10 each produce a total revenue of £10,000 (£10 × 1,000). There are fixed costs of £2,500 which remain unchanged throughout the period of producing from 0 to 1,000 units. Variable costs totalling £5 per unit are shown in addition to fixed costs and total (£5 × 1,000) £5,000. The break-even point occurs at 500 units and the profit upon 1,000 units sold is £2,500. In this commercial situation the margin of safety – the difference between the break-even point and the total sales forecast of 1,000 units – is 500 units.

Example B

In Example B (Figure 4.3) precisely the same figures are used except that the fixed and variable cost amounts have been revised. Although the total costs and the total revenues remain the same at £7,500 and £10,000 respectively, the break-even point has been increased from 500 units to 675. Such a revision will be all too familiar to a manufacturer who has contracted to supply a given number of units to a customer at an initial fixed price, but between agreeing the price and supplying the units variable and sometimes fixed costs have risen. The commercial risk in Example B is higher than A despite exactly similar profitability. Why? Because more sales have to be made to reach the break-even point.

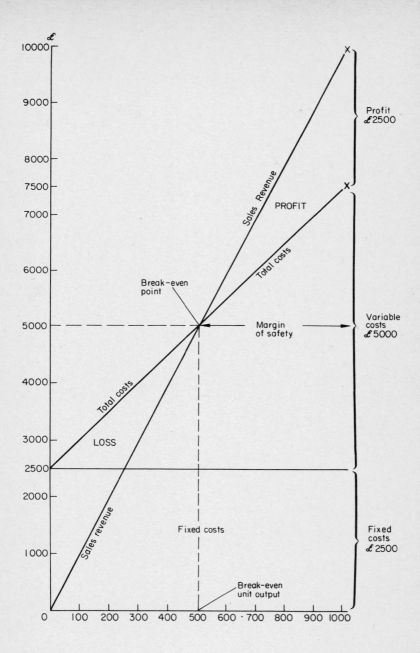

Figure 4.2   Example A

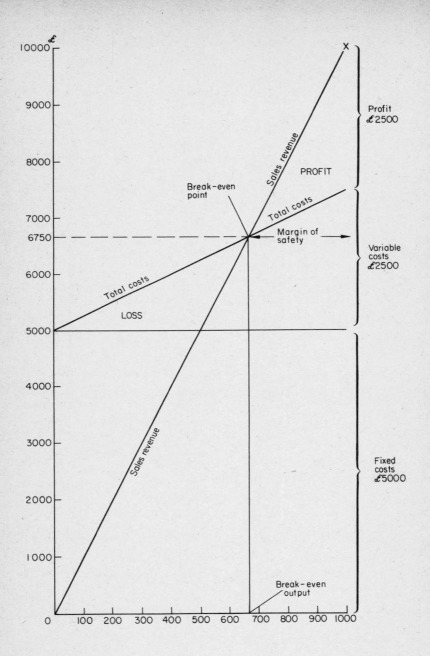

Figure 4.3 Example B

50

Example C

Historically many companies based (and some still do) the price of their products on a 'cost plus' approach. This is arrived at simply and mathematically by adding up all the costs involved in making a product and then dividing this figure by the quantity of products actually produced or planned to be produced. To the resulting figure management then adds a marginal figure, hence the term 'cost plus'; but this approach does not help a company to answer the question of whether to accept or reject additional orders over and above those they have planned to produce. So it is necessary to have a 'market' approach to pricing products and services which enables a company to judge, once fixed costs have been covered, whether marginal business, which can make a contribution to the company's sales turnover, is worth accepting or rejecting.

Some businesses prefer to plot variable costs before fixed costs on a break-even chart. This is so that the contribution can be graphically shown and illustrates what is known as the 'marginal costing' approach. In Example C (Figure 4.4) the same figures as in A have been used.

The gap marked 'X' between the revenue and variable cost lines is in fact 'contribution': it is therefore possible to see, for example, that when 250 units have been sold, although no profit has been made, all the variable costs thus far have been covered and 50 per cent of the fixed costs have been paid off. Such a cross reference between sales and their contribution to meeting fixed costs cannot easily be made from the more traditional form of break-even graph.

Example D

The break-even chart is flexible enough to cope not only with changes in revenue and costs but to feed back the impact of such changes in terms of profit and loss positions of a manufacturing project. In Example D (Figure 4.5) fixed costs starting at £2,500 remain so until 750 units when they increase, perhaps due to having to buy a larger delivery van. But variable costs from 750 units have been reduced slightly which could be due to being able to bulk more orders into each delivery, giving a saving in transport costs. There is a flattening out of the revenue line from 1,050 units, which indicates that the final few sales have been made at reduced prices.

There are now, as a result of changes during production in the amount of fixed and variable costs, two break-even points, one at about 525 units the other at 900 units, and thus two profit areas, indicated as shaded sections.

Such a chart indicates the various volumes at which profit is made.

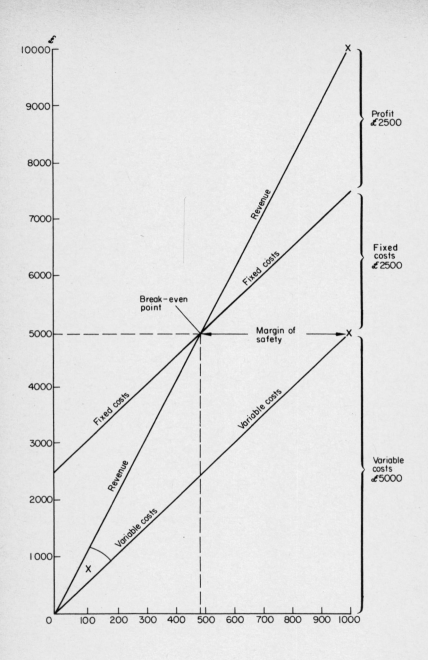

Figure 4.4   Example C

52

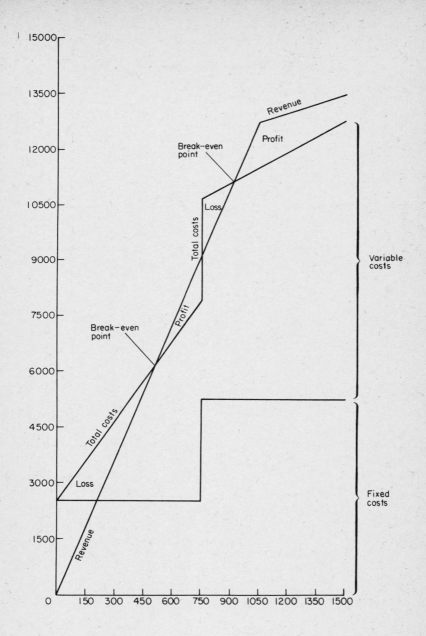

Figure 4.5 Example D

For example at 749 units the profit is about £1,200 but a comparable amount does not recur until sales have reached 1,050 units and even then the profit is likely to be a little over £1,100. Such a break-even graph indicates that if the company sells between 749 and 900 units it will make less than if it only sold 749 units. This example shows the use of a break-even chart for indicating such relationships, particularly as is common in more and more manufacturing companies where revenue and cost patterns change over the span of projected unit sales against which production targets and output have been based. Ever since the dramatic and frequent rises in the price of crude oil, the majority of companies throughout the world have had to check changes in fixed and variable costs sometimes daily and certainly weekly to have any hope of keeping break-even targets in sight by constant adjustments (always upwards!) in their prices, as we all know to our cost.

Conclusion

The break-even chart is a useful device for presenting a picture of cost/volume/profit relationships, to show the effects of changes in various factors such as *volume sales*, *price* and *costs*.

One of the major problems of the break-even chart is that the revenue line assumes a constant product mix, i.e. that ten units of sales are always worth the same amount of revenue. In single product companies, and even those producing a range of different products where the mix is easily controlled and assumptions about revenue line can be made, care must be exercised otherwise the chart becomes unrealistic.

In negotiating with large buyers where pricing can be flexible beyond the break-even area, the chart provides key account salesmen and marketing colleagues with a basis for assessing tactical marketing situations or propositions such as various forms of promotional activity, different methods of sales compensation to the sales force, to agents, distributors, etc.

When used in this way the break-even chart can provide a graphical basis for assessing profit and risk and so help key account negotiators to make such decisions on behalf of their own companies and in discussions with buyers.

Appendix to Part One

All businesses face increasing commercial pressures. One of your prime responsibilities must be to assist your customers in creating and using profit opportunities through the use of your products or services.

Financial knowledge is an important selling tool to help you in achieving your objectives. It will be essential in the future for all business negotiators to understand the nature of profit and the factors affecting the commercial success of both their own and their customers' businesses.

The following check-lists will help you to assess your own financial knowledge and awareness and enable you to identify how best you can develop financial selling skills as an aid to profitable long-term sales. By asking these questions and by quantifying the answers you can establish how you can improve your customers' financial returns, how you can translate the improvements into benefits which he will understand and accept, and how you can communicate them to him effectively – more effectively than your competitors.

Financial knowledge: Check-list

	Yes	No	Action
Do I have a basic knowledge of finance in business?			
Do I understand the nature of the following and the influence of my activities on them?			
The balance sheet			
The profit and loss account			
Sources of capital			
Uses of capital			
Fixed assets			
Current assets			
Long-term liabilities			
Short term liabilities			

	Yes	No	Action
Capital employed			
Sales revenue			
Profit			
Return on sales ratio			
Sales to capital employed ratio			
Return on capital employed ratio			
Cash flow			
Fixed costs			
Variable costs			
Contribution			

Internal financial needs: Check-list

In evaluating your own selling activity you can apply the same criteria as for checking your own financial knowledge. The results of your selling activity have considerable implications both for return on sales and sales: capital employed.

	Yes	No	Action
Return on sales			
(a) Are we selling our targeted volume?			
(b) Are we achieving target prices?			
(c) Are we giving away excessive or unnecessary concessions?			
(d) Are we achieving the targeted mix?			
(e) Are we looking at our selling costs relative to volume?			
(f) Do we make full creative use of expenditure on sales support activities?			
(g) Are we being cost-effective as salesmen?			
(h) Can we quantify our activities in terms of costs and opportunities?			

	Yes	No	Action

Sales:capital employed

(a) Are we selling our targeted volume?

(b) Do our forecasts accurately reflect future sales?

(c) What effect do wrong forecasts have on capital tied up in stocks and the cost of stocks?

(d) Are we keeping debtors to targeted levels?

(e) Are we using our time and expenditure to achieve effective new sales?

(f) Can we quantify our activity in terms of the relationship between sales and capital employed?

(g) Are we keeping stock levels too high to make selling 'easier' (but no more effective)?

(h) Are we selling factory capacity?

Customer financial needs: Check-list

	Know	Don't know	Action

How is the customer's business structured in financial terms?

What financial ratios are crucial to his business?

How can our products or services improve his results?

How can these be quantified?

1 Improve return : sales ratio

   (a) reduce production, marketing, administrative or distribution costs;

(b)   make functions more cost effective;

(c)   increase sales volume;

(d)   increase sales revenue;

(e)   improve margins;

(f)   add value to his products;

(g)   achieve larger unit sales/better sales mix.

2   Improve sales: capital employed ratio

(a)   increase production sales;

(b)   reduce stocks of finished goods or raw materials;

(c)   reduce debtors?

(d)   speed through-put/stock turnover?

(e)   reduce need for cash?

(f)   make better use of fixed assets?

(g)   reduce machinery costs?

(h)   reduce labour costs?

(i)   make better use of space?

(j)   reduce distribution costs?

PART II
NEGOTIATION TECHNIQUES

Introduction to Part II

Negotiation, or the art of bargaining, is, like selling, as old as the history of mankind. But unlike selling, it has either not had the spotlight focused upon it or the art of negotiation has not been considered a fit or worthy subject for authorship. Whatever the reason, there is a dearth of reference material and very little in the way of practical guidelines to help today's sales negotiators.

Yet if we took the trouble to study the arts of diplomacy we should find that they are one and the same as business negotiation. The following extracts from *The Perfect Diplomat*, and other sayings, should be read to illumine your thinking and to show that there is nothing new in business; the secret of success, as in most other spheres of life, is the ability to predict when the pattern of events must repeat itself. Otherwise as the German philosopher Hegel said:
'We learn from history that we do *not* learn from history.'

'Diplomacy is the art of getting what we want.'
'We distinguish good diplomacy from bad by the results obtained and the price paid.'
'Official diplomacy must carry on in the world as it is, not in the world as it should be.'
'Things are sometimes what they seem, but rarely what they are called.'
'A diplomat sometimes has to deal with people who appear to be stupid. Very often they are stupid. But it is better not to count on their stupidity.'
'A diplomat should be a realist without being a cynic.'
'Sometimes it is possible to win, if we are content not to triumph.'
'If you overdo propaganda, you may find that nothing fails like success.'
'There is nothing so good or so bad that you will not find an Englishman doing it. But you will never find an Englishman in the wrong. He does everything on principle.'
'The Chinese when discussing a political controversy will not seek out moral issues but ask only: "On what basis will the combatants come to terms?" For this is what it amounts to in the end.'
'Like a bullet, a diplomat will go farthest if he is smooth.'
'Our [diplomatic] arts are the immemorial devices of the peasant in the market place, buying and selling his wares.'
'Machiavelli said: "When doing good do it little by little. When doing evil, do it all at once." '

'In 1873 Bismarck said: "If you want to buy a horse, you will not shout from the roof-tops the highest price you would consent to pay for it; and if you want to sell a horse, you will not begin by admitting publicly the lowest price that you would be content to accept. Diplomacy must show no less restraint." '
(Extracts from *The Handbook of the Perfect Diplomat*, written in 1929 by Daniele Varé)

Adam Smith, the 17th-century economist, said: 'Man is an animal that makes bargains; no other animal does this – no dog exchanges bones with another.'

Lord Home said: 'Remember to ask yourself before you act what the effect is likely to be on the other fellow.'

5 Why negotiation?

Many buyer–supplier relationships which salesmen have traditionally regarded as 'selling' situations have changed considerably over the last ten to fifteen years. These changes and their effect on the role and relationships between buyer and seller need to be understood if salesmen are to operate successfully in the market place described in Chapter 1.

In recent years the distributive trades and major industrial, service and financial customers have developed their own marketing and business expertise and with it their own commercial strategies and plans. Among the major distributors in the grocery and food markets are many groups whose marketing skills are equal to, if not more advanced than, some of the major food manufacturers who supply them. In the opening chapter reference was made to other factors that have changed, the most important of which is the considerable concentration of buying power into fewer but larger purchasing units.

These developments, greater buying expertise and greater buyer power, have led to an increased amount of interdependence between manufacturers or suppliers and distributor or users. Although the two sides still occasionally make independent warlike noises there is a growing amount of tacit recognition that they need each other if they are to achieve their respective commercial objectives. This relationship and interdependence calls for a subtle understanding by the salesman of the skills he needs and when he should use them.

In terms of 'selling' activity this means that there is a greater balance of needs on both sides. The need to buy and the need to supply, viewed over a period of time, are more or less equal.

'Negotiation' is the term generally applied to the more complex situations involving buyers and sellers, in which both make a number of proposals and counter proposals before an agreement is reached. 'Persuasive selling' is still needed, particularly with new customers, in the more competitive industries (e.g. food groups) or when presenting a new product or idea. But given commonality of needs in the majority of cases between buyer and seller, it is the greater skill of negotiation that is required to ensure the business gained is profitable.

The nature of sales technique

Traditionally 'selling' is seen as the art and skill of persuading someone who at the outset of a sales interview is reluctant to buy that he should do so. To achieve this sales objective, the salesman uses a repertoire of techniques by means of which he raises the customer's perception of the need to buy to a point where he acts upon that need.

There are many different approaches to the structuring of sales techniques, some of the most simple approaches used by salesmen tell us about the seller's needs, e.g.:

1 Opening questions or statements about a customer's needs, designed to pin-point need or raise perception of it.
2 Presentation of benefits based on identified needs, designed to raise desire in the customer's mind for these benefits.
3 Handling and overcoming objections raised by customer, designed to remove obstacles that could prevent the customer from buying.
4 Closing the sale, designed to get the customer to say 'yes' and buy.

Other approaches tell us more about the customer's needs, e.g.:

1 I am important and want to be respected.
2 Consider my needs.
3 Will your ideas help me?
4 What are the facts?
5 What are the snags?
6 What shall I do?
7 I approve.

Whatever the approach, the objective in terms of the end result is to increase the customer's need for the salesman's products, services or ideas to a level where to satisfy that need he states the decision to buy. If you examine the movement of the two parties involved (seller and buyer) in these sales approaches, you can see that the salesman's need to sell is much greater than the buyer's need to buy. Indeed he uses selling as a process of inducing the buyer to move to a position where the buyer's need for the product or service coincides with the need of the salesman to sell it to him. Although the salesman frequently goes physically to see a buyer to sell to him, his sales proposition is often inflexible. The salesman in this sense does not move. He uses selling as a means of inducing or 'motivating' the buyer to *move* (see Figure 5.1).

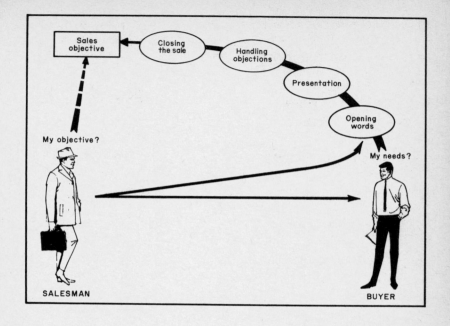

Figure 5.1   Stepping stones in a sale

What is selling?

It is the relationship between supplier and buyer (or potential buyer) where the need to supply significantly exceeds the need to buy. Thus selling is the *persuasive* process by which a supplier aims to convince a buyer of his need for his (the supplier's) product or service and the buyer acts upon that need.

Strength of a company's need to sell

In a good many companies the persuasive sales approach is always used. Sometimes this is not only understandable but appropriate. For example, a new, unknown company, starting out in business to market a product or a service which may be original or a duplicate of product or services already available, has to make known its existence and then to use all its powers of persuasion to get people to buy its products or use its services.

Strength of salesman's need to sell

Another and less defensible reason for maintaining the persuasive sales approach is that in some businesses where, in terms of results achieved over a period of years, it has been highly successful, the salesman's need to sell, to persuade, to win is invariably high. This need has usually been present to a marked degree in the individual members of the sales force when they were recruited. Indeed the presence of this need was an essential ingredient for sales success, heightened by skilfully structured sales training.

But to pursue this approach to business development without assessing its relevance can be dangerous because it may lead to the salesman making general assumptions about the customer's low need to buy which are not true. They assume that the customer avoids buying decisions wherever possible by deploying supposedly unreal objections. One highly successful international group pioneered the development of photocopying, created excellent products and built up a formidable market share through aggressive salesmanship. Now that its photo-copying machine patents have come to an end, other companies have entered this lucrative market offering identical or improved versions of the pioneer's successful machines. So success in pioneering a market led to others entering it with the loss of product superiority which in the past had provided effective answers to the question: 'Why should I buy from you?'

To continue to use a traditional sales approach in such a situation when the buyer's need to buy can almost be taken for granted, would not only be inappropriate but, when dealing with a sharp buyer, very costly. It could be said that, given a good product or service, plus the application of sustained salesmanship, has produced a position where the buyer no longer needs convincing of whether he should buy but rather has to consider *on what basis he should buy*. This is the stage at which negotiation takes over from selling and presents a quite different challenge to the traditionally trained salesman. This is the stage when the salesman's heightened need 'to sell' often expressed in the adoption of simple objectives for the sale situation, can be counter-productive: for example, the salesman plans to get an order at every call, on the assumption that to get one indicates success and not to secure an order would be classified as failure. When the relationship between buyer and seller becomes one of *negotiating* and not selling, it will either blossom or deteriorate, dependent upon the salesman's capacity or incapacity to perceive that this selling situation is different from the past. This is where the temptation to fall back on yesterday's training or experiences to find satisfactory solutions to today's customer behaviour is understandable but ineffective. The salesman is no longer engaging in a persuasive tug-of-war with the customer in which one of them wins; and so far as the salesman is concerned the evidence of victory is an order whatever the cost to get it. In negotiation there are no losers – both win.

The circumstances which surround negotiation

Successful sales techniques produce the basis for any negotiation. By sales technique the customer is moved to a position where, in order to satisfy his now heightened perception of his need, he considers the purchase decision. He then turns his attention to the *terms and conditions* of the sales and purchase.

Having been satisfied during the selling phase that the product or service has benefits which meet his needs (as adequately or more so than those offered by competitors), the customer then focuses more closely upon the many detailed factors surrounding the decision. The whole emphasis moves towards the *profit* implications of the decision. This is the most marked difference between selling and negotiation – the nature of the end result for both sides. In selling we are concerned with benefits related to products or services. In negotiation we are motivated by the effect on the profitability or reduction in costs to both sides of the outcome of our discussions. The buyer will be asking detailed questions on these subjects:

1 *Actual price:*

    (a) what is the price?
    (b) what discounts/interest rates? (if negotiating with a bank manager);
    (c) what additional bonuses/reductions?
    (d) when will I have to pay?

2 *Actual product:*

    (a) what pack sizes?
    (b) what order size?
    (c) back up stock/recommended parts levels to be carried?

3 *Allied services:*

    (a) when do I want it delivered?
    (b) at what rate do I want it delivered?
    (c) how much distributive cost can I avoid?

(d) what technical support will I need in using the product?
(e) how can I avoid paying extra for it?
(f) what advertising/merchandising/support?

Based on the platform of a need both to buy and supply created by selling, the give-and-take process can start, whereby the final detailed terms and conditions surrounding the purchase/supply decision are agreed.

In this phase we are tailoring the details of the product, price and presentation to fit the immediate needs of one particular customer. Because of this we and the purchaser are involved in *compromise*. This element of controlled compromise (which must be recognised to ensure profit) often clashes with the uncompromising inflexible nature of many sales techniques.

Having achieved that phase the salesman must then leave the security of his fixed position and bring about the final agreement by moving and *appearing to move* towards the customer and inducing reciprocal movement from the customer.

It is recognising this situation that is the critical step. Once recognised, we can ensure each move we make costs the supplier as little as possible, and gains as much as possible in the movement by the customer.

What is negotiation?

The relationship between supplier and buyer where the need to supply is largely in balance with the need to buy. It is taken as self-evident, therefore, in a negotiation that in the final analysis the buyer needs your products because he makes his profit by meeting his customer needs, and your products enable him to do that. For obvious reasons these facts are rarely discussed (or admitted) during negotiation, but they form an essential, implicit bed-rock for discussions.

The commercial role of negotiation

Given a commonality of needs over a period of time, it does not automatically follow that a customer will buy on every occasion, or to the level which the manufacturer would prefer.

Whether or not the supplier actively features a product and promotes its sale will depend largely upon the terms and conditions of the 'deal' under consideration. (Interestingly 'to deal' means 'to bargain or negotiate or attempt to come to terms'.)

Negotiation, then, is the give and take process whereby the actual conditions of a transaction are agreed. It is the process where agreement is reached on product/service range and volume, technical advice, prices, promotional support, delivery, payment terms, and where mutual satisfaction is achieved.

The buyer's perspective

In looking at the nature of negotiation it is important to understand the needs and perspectives of the buyer. The nature of negotiation from the buyer's perspective has been well defined in instructions issued to United States Air Force buying personnel.

'Procurement by negotiation is the art of arriving at a common understanding through bargaining on the essentials of a contract such as delivery, specifications, prices and terms. Because of the interrelation of these factors with many others, it is a difficult art and requires the exercise of judgement, tact and commonsense. The effective negotiator must be a real shopper, alive to the possibilities of bargaining with the seller. Only through the awareness of relative bargaining strength can a negotiator know where to be firm or where he may make permissive concessions in prices or terms.' Air Force Procurement Instructions 3 – 102 50.

The ingredients of his negotiation needs will be a combination of:

1 Profit margins (if a distributor?).
2 Price (but rarely in isolation).
3 Quality (in his terms).
4 Product range/specification/etc. (to meet the needs of his customers).
5 Cost (in real not purchase terms).
6 Availability.
7 Brand name (his own or the suppliers).
8 Proof of value (in his terms, e.g. the speed with which promotional quantities will sell out).
9 The output of a machine.

Negotiation should therefore be seen by both parties as the process of working out a procurement and sales problem together to reach mutually satisfactory agreement. Knowledge and skill in negotiation is an important asset to the negotiator. It must include knowledge of:

1 Cost/value assessment.

2   Ability to marshal facts logically and convincingly and to deal with people effectively when under pressure.
3   At the same time the buyer must be helped to understand your position. No major purchasing programme can be stronger than the sources of supply – ultimately both parties are mutually dependent.

Price perspective

In particular it is useful to examine the professional buyer's view of price in relation to other factors. He must aim to get his company into the best position in the buying hierarchy. It gives him a competitive advantage. Price, obviously, is of importance to him but rarely in isolation. It is important for him to relate price to value because his investment in the deal is less important than the investment in the *return* from that deal. Paradoxically he is often judged by his management on his price negotiating skills, yet even he will talk of 'price buyers' in derogatory terms. He must, therefore, achieve the best balance for his company. Good buyers are trained to resist questionably low prices because of the inherent risks, for example, of quality, reliability, delivery and service. Where industry pricing is common, or is influenced by limited competition when a market is shared by a small number of manufacturers or suppliers, buyers seek to negotiate the conditions of purchase.

Conclusion

In this chapter so far we have defined and examined the differences between *negotiation* and *selling*. An acute understanding of this difference and of the buyer's perspective is essential to the salesman in developing his key-customer plans, his approach and his tactics. Ultimately the best negotiator will not only achieve his own and his customer's objectives but he will also be more successful than his competitors.

If a salesman uses selling techniques in a meeting with a key buyer who is not only *professionally trained to negotiate* but is also *a competent negotiator*, the chances will always be tilted in favour of the buyer winning and the salesman losing although the latter may obtain an order or increase the percentage volume of business being transacted.

The following interview between a skilled buyer and a salesman using *traditional selling techniques* illustrates all too vividly just how costly the eventual order he obtains is – to his company.

Example of a traditionally trained salesman selling to a highly skilled buyer

The commercial situation

The buyer. Mr Johnson is the professional buyer of a large, well-known firm of plant and plant-hire contractors. His company operates machines ranging from small mechanically driven road-rollers to the largest industrial earth-moving equipment. He has asked a major plant manufacturer with whom his company has done business in the past to quote for the supply of an initial order of ten motorway construction machines. The list purchase price of each machine is £11,500, and not unnaturally for an order of this size the buyer has invited other manufacturers to tender. Mr Johnson has been trained in finance and purchasing.

The salesman. Mr Edmunds is an experienced salesman who has a background of factory experience. He was given a basic sales training course before taking over a sales territory. He is considered by his company to be a competent and reasonably successful member of the twelve-man sales force. He has done a small amount of business in the past with Mr Johnson and has recently had a number of discussions with both operating and technical staff to obtain the necessary information needed to prepare the quotation to supply the ten machines.

Buyer's objectives

To obtain the best possible machines for his company on time to meet his company's financial and marketing plans. This company's machines are of the best quality and he will try and negotiate their purchase on the following terms:

1 To obtain the machines with the guarantee that 'C' part spares stock

Salesman's objectives

To sell ten new machines at the quotation price.

1 To arrange for the machines to be delivered to Birmingham within the price allowed for in the quotation.
2 To supply the recommended parts stock to the level specified in the quotation.
3 To ensure that arrangements are made to train

Buyer's objective	Salesman's objective

unused are taken back by the manufacturer at the end of twelve months free of charge.

the new machine operators to correspond with the dates of delivery.

2 To have the machines painted in the company's new livery free of charge.

3 To have the machines delivered to a number of different depots rather than all to one and so avoid carrying the cost of onward delivery.

4 To have the operators and fitters responsible for the new machines trained on a special course laid on by the manufacturer free of charge.

5 To obtain the manufacturer's agreement in writing to a guaranteed buy-back figure.

6 To obtain a discount of 2½ per cent off the quoted price of each machine.

The costs involved in the transaction

1 Quoted price of machines: £11,500 each: $10 \times £11,500 =$ £115,000.

2 Initial cost of recommended parts stock: £4,100 ('C' part spares value £2,800).

3 Cost of paint-spraying each machine: £35 per machine.

4   Cost of delivering ten machines to one point (Birmingham): £700.

5   Cost of delivering to separate points: minimum £100 per machine to a distance of 100 miles from plant (any distance over that 50p per mile extra).

6   Cost of operator training at company's training school: £35 per delegate.

The discussion		*Notes*
Buyer	Good morning Mr Edmunds, please sit down.	
Salesman	Thank you Mr Johnson. You have our quote I see.	
B	Yes, thank you very much.	
S	I hope you have found it interesting.	Salesman tests buyer's attitude to the quotation.
B	Oh yes, indeed. Not quite so good as some of the others I have received but nevertheless interesting.	Buyer emphasises that other quotations are better, thus putting the salesman under pressure.
S	Oh! Which specific points were not as satisfactory as you might have liked.	Salesman rightly attempts to clarify the buyer's remark.
B	Well technically I think it's quite good in the sense that from our discussions last time you obviously understood our technical requirements very well and I have no quibbles in that direction. However, we are of course purchasing a total system and not just a machine. We are purchasing all the bits and pieces that go with it, commissioning and everything else and I think it is in that area that you need to have a closer look.	Buyer begins to soften up the salesman.

The discussion	Notes
S Where were there any particular problems that you saw?	Salesman seeks further clarification.
B Well I think they are several areas, perhaps we should take them one at a time. Let's deal first of all with this question of parts stock. Now in your quotation you put a recommended parts-stock level, which is normal practice. But of course in this particular case we are talking about ten machines and also talking about a brand-new model and inevitably I think you put in a recommended parts stock which both in terms of quantity and value is relatively high compared with standard situations, and that of course is going to involve us in a considerable financial commitment and one which quite frankly I am reluctant to accept at this point in time. So what I would like you to do is to have another look at the recommended parts level, and in those cases where we don't use them during the first twelve months to come to some arrangement whereby you will take these back free of charge.	Buyer prefers to deal with one thing at a time and in the sequence of his choice. Starts with first point: *Parts stock.*
	Buyer emphasises the cost of carrying the recommended parts stock.
	Buyer asks for a concession on parts stock.

The discussion	Notes

<table>
<tr><td>S</td><td>Yes, I see we're talking about the 'C' class spares are we?</td><td>Salesman clarifies.</td></tr>
<tr><td>B</td><td>That's right and there were some of them which are not common to other machines, and it is those that I am concerned about.</td><td></td></tr>
<tr><td>S</td><td>Yes.</td><td></td></tr>
<tr><td>B</td><td>I don't think these will present you with any difficulty will they?</td><td>Buyer minimises the effect of the concession on the supplier.</td></tr>
<tr><td>S</td><td>Well the warranty will cover a fair amount of that and at the end of twelve months it may be that you are buying new machines and will need to balance the parts stock up, or otherwise I am sure we can produce a buy-back situation with no problem.</td><td>Salesman partly concedes.</td></tr>
<tr><td>B</td><td>Good, fine. Now that covers the area of the recommended parts stock. Another point which we need to talk about is the question of livery.
I think I mentioned to you last time when we were talking about the technical specification that we have in fact been doing an analysis of our corporate image.</td><td>Buyer confirms the concession. He now turns to his second point: Livery.</td></tr>
<tr><td>S</td><td>Yes.</td><td></td></tr>
<tr><td>B</td><td>That analysis has now been completed and as a result what we are going to have to do is change various</td><td></td></tr>
</table>

parts of our corporate
image. You know at the
bottom end it involves very
simple things like
changing our letterheads
and so on. It also means
developing the speaking
abilities of our people
who take hirings over the
telephone. But one major
area where we are going to
have to make a change is
livery. We are currently
repainting all our existing
fleet and with the addition
of these new machines into
the fleet what I am going   Buyer asks for concession.
to need is for them to be
delivered to us in the
new colours.

S   That wasn't in fact in the   Salesman resists.
    original specification.

B   No, I am sorry about that   Buyer apologises, but
    but at that time of course   repeats his request.
    we hadn't completed our
    analysis. So what I would
    like you to do is arrange
    for these ten machines to
    be painted in our new
    colours prior to delivery
    to us.

S   Is the basic paint job
    apart from stencils still
    yellow?

B   Yellow will still be in the
    colours but the
    predominant colour now
    will be green, Lincoln
    green.

S   I see. I think we can   Salesman agrees to the
    arrange that without too   change.

much problem. You can let
us have the exact code of
the paint and the
necessary artwork and so
on, some stills of
existing machines?

B   Yes indeed. And as what   Buyer requests it FOC.
normally happens you will
of course do this free of
charge?

S   Yes, we can I think accom-   Salesman agrees.
modate that. There's no
particular problem there
and you want these then
delivered through to   Buyer's third point:
Birmingham?   *Delivery*.

B   Yes, certainly three of   Buyer has changed his
them will be required in   original delivery
Birmingham, but we want   requirements.
the others delivered to
our other regional depots.

S   Mmm, I thought all ten
were going through to
Birmingham?

B   This indeed was our
original thinking. However,
we have looked at the
situation again and we
have had discussions with
our various regional
managers and they have
expressed the view that
there is a demand for
these machines in their
own areas. In addition we
feel that we would like to
get some idea of how the
machines perform under
different geographic
conditions, and also
because if these machines

are successful we will
probably want to increase
the fleet at regular
intervals, we need to
sound out the demand in
particular areas to see
where extra machines
should go. Now this means
that of the ten three will
be required in Birmingham,
(you know where our
Birmingham depot is, very
close to you at Wolver-
hampton). Three will be
required in London and
I'll give you the details.

S I know the London depot
well.

B Well as you know it's at
the bottom of the motorway
so that's no problem. Two
will be required in
Manchester and our
Manchester depot is about
four miles off the
Altrincham turn-off on the
M6. One is required in
Glasgow and one is
required in Plymouth, and
I imagine, of course, that
you do make deliveries
from time to time in
these areas so this won't
present any particular
problem.

S They are quite widely
spread.

B Indeed, I think I should
add that in the
competitive quotes that we
have had, delivery to

Buyer suggests possible
future business as a
lever to obtain a
delivery concession.

Buyer minimises incon-
venience and cost of
change in delivery
specification.

Buyer continues to
minimise the cost and
inconvenience of the
geographic delivery
scheduling of these
machines.

Buyer makes salesman feel
uncompetitive.

these depots has been
offered by the companies
concerned.

S Free delivery?

B Oh indeed, yes.

S Then I think that we will   Salesman agrees to
have to make sure that   concession.
that's done for you.

B Thank you.

S Fine (and makes a note as
does the buyer).

B Now one point I wanted to   Buyer raises fourth point:
raise with you was the   *Operator training.*
date of the training
courses when you're going
to send our people into
Wolverhampton.

S Yes. You'll be sending ten
people into Wolverhampton
for the operator training
course?

B Not quite. We have as far
as operators are concerned
between two or three
people at each of the
regional centres who will
require training, so we're
talking about twelve or
fifteen people. We also
feel that it is important
that the people who have
to maintain these
machines are also made
familiar with their
operation.

S Yes.

B That being the case, what
we want to do is to train
both the operators and the
fitters. So this means we
are talking in total of

twenty/twenty-five people.

S   Well normally we offer a
    training for one person
    per machine.

B   Yes.

S   One operator per machine.

B   Yes.

S   And we don't really want   Salesman explains situ-
    to overload the training   ation on training.
    school. The school
    obviously has a limited
    number of places, limited
    amount of courses and
    numbers of lecturers, and
    we find that the training
    centre has been set up in
    fact to match the demands
    that are made on it
    against the sales forecast
    that we make on machines.

B   Yes, I appreciate that
    because we have of course
    sent people on previous
    occasions where we have
    bought one-off items from
    you in the past. Now
    I have looked at this and
    I think there is one way
    that we can get round this   Buyer minimises the cost
    which will cause you the   to the supplier of his
    minimum of inconvenience.   proposition.
    What I would like to do
    is to pull them all
    together as a group. Now
    this, of course, will
    present problems to you on
    your normal programmes.
    So what I am going to
    suggest is that we pull
    them all together at one
    of our depots and

obviously the most con-
venient one is Birmingham,
because that's closest to
you and your own training
centre.

S   Yes.

B   We will provide the accommodation facilities, we
will provide the training
environment, we will make
everything just as you
want it. All you would
need to do is to lay on
the trainer and because,
by the time we do the
training the machines that
we need won't have been
delivered to the regional
centres, I would like you
to lay on a demonstration
training machine as well.
So all you would need to   Buyer makes his request
do is to provide the   seem very reasonable.
trainer and to provide the
machine and we'll provide
the environment and everything else and the accom-
modation.

S   So what you are really
saying is that instead of
sending ten people in, you
want the increased number
of operators and fitters in
your own location with
the machine?

B   Yes. Let me elaborate on   Buyer emphasises the size
that. This is a large   of the order to soften
purchase by any standards.   up the salesman.
As you well know, on
training programmes which
are attended by people

from various companies you have, inevitably people talk, and in fact I believe that this is a training method in which you do in fact encourage people to exchange experience. With the standards of maintenance that we have, and our methods of maintenance, I am very reluctant indeed to expose those to fitters and operators from competitive companies. In other words I don't want this to get about well before the machines are available because some of our competitors may well take action to prevent us getting the level of business that we shall need for these machines. So that is another reason why I would like to pull all these people together under one roof and have this programme specifically for us.

Buyer 'sells' his proposal.

S   Well I will have to check it with my training centre to make sure that they do have a machine available because the machines are in great demand. But I would think if they will give it the O.K. we can promise you that and we can put that together. That will be in early December?

Salesman conditionally agrees.

The discussion

B I would think so. Of course we're not putting any strain on your training centre or its programme.

S No, quite. So really we must look at the parts stock and get a guarantee buy-back there; the paint job; delivery to those centres and we will organise that special training for you. Can we then go ahead on that basis?

B Almost. Almost. I think we're almost there Mr Edmunds. There's just one area that I would like to tidy up before we make a decision, and even if we do tidy it up I think I should emphasise that I've still got to look at the other ones as well. As you know it has always been our policy in the past to hold our machines for a length of time and then to sell them off.

S Yes.

B Now this policy runs counter to the policies of many companies who hold the machines for a period and then under a buy-back arrangement that they have with the manufacturer the machines are taken back by the manufacturer at an

Notes

Salesman tries to close.

Buyer, having already obtained a number of valuable concessions, tries for another: *Buy-back agreement.*

agreed price. Now what I
would like to do in this
particular situation,
because these are new
models, is to have that
arrangement with you, so
that we will forego our
normal procedure of
selling them off and come
to some arrangement now
whereby we have a buy-
back agreement.

S   Of course you are quite   Salesman answers.
right we do have buy-back
arrangements, though
normally that is with
contractor's own plant.
The problem with plant
hire, quite simply, is that
the conditions are very
variable, and the effect on
a machine that works, for
example, purely on
overburden instead of high
silica sand, can be quite
different, which has a
major effect on its value.
In addition to which I
think that when you
sometimes simply hire the
machine you don't always
hire it out with an
operator, and that of
course, also as you know
very well, with some of
the cowboys they have
about, has an effect. I
think the company would
be very reluctant to
guarantee a buy-back,
especially since this is a

new machine and we're
not quite sure of the
demand levels in the
present economic
situation.

B   Yes, I think you'll find,
however, there are more
cowboys amongst the general
contractors than there are
amongst plant-hire people.

> Buyer counters the
> salesman's argument.

S   Indeed yes. Yes, the point
I was making was that if
you do hire out machines
without an operator then
that is where the misuse
so often takes place.

> Salesman rephrases his
> explanation.

B   I'm sorry, you misunderstand me. With the
contractor, practically all
the time the machines are
being operated by the
cowboys, whereas with us,
where we hire out for
most of the time with an
operator, the machine is
under very close control. I
think there are other
considerations as well,
which I think would
influence your view here.
One is that on many
occasions we are hiring
out for lengthy periods to
people whom we know in
conditions with which we
are familiar, and we know
perfectly well that the
machine is going to be
well maintained and the
conditions are not going
to be arduous. That's one

> Buyer counters again.

consideration. The other is
that in plant hire we have
the ultimate sanction as to
whether we take a hire or
not.

S   Yes.

B   And, of course, one of the
major considerations in
taking a hire or not is the
conditions under which
that machine is going to
be operated. Now for
those reasons I think that
what you are likely to
find, particularly bearing
in mind our regular
maintenance which we
have to carry out in order
to maintain the level of
service that our customers
need, also bearing in mind
the corporate image I am
talking about, that under
most circumstances these
machines are operated and
maintained to a fairly high
standard and therefore
buy-back under these
circumstances should be
relatively easy for you.

S   Yes, I can see that that
is so. The real problem of
course is that it would be
very difficult for you at
the stage we agreed the   Salesman resists buyer's
buy-back level to, in   pressure to agree a
fact, tell us what those   buy-back price for the
conditions were going to   machines.
be. Therefore we have a
difficult situation of
projecting exactly what

that would be. At this
stage my company would
not be able to produce a
settled buy-back figure.
That really would be very
difficult for us.

B You're saying that doing it
in advance creates great
problems because you
don't know what the
circumstances are going to
be?

S Really yes.

B Well perhaps we can
approach it from another
angle. I take it that your
company is interested in
this business?

S Oh indeed, yes certainly.

B Now that being the case,
as an alternative if you
can't do buy-back, and
I must say I am very
disappointed that you
don't feel you can do
anything along these lines,
but as an alternative what
we could consider is some
form of discount off the
purchase price that you
have quoted.

S Well, as you know, the
price that we put in
originally was very keen.
You are quite right we are
very interested in getting
this business indeed and I
don't know that we have a
great deal of leeway at the
price we quoted.

B Yes your price is keen,

Buyer has to accept
salesman's answer, so he
switches to a price
objection.

Buyer makes salesman feel
he is being reasonable.

Buyer puts salesman's

but I think that you should know that it has been bettered.

S   Well what particular levels of discount are we talking about?

B   Well I would imagine that while they've been tested, their performance still needs to be proved long term. With this type of machine in this kind of situation I would say that something in the order of 4½ per cent would be acceptable to me.

S   4½ per cent is a great deal of money. It's coming considerably outside my court. At this stage I am quite sure that we will find it very difficult to stretch to 4½. That really is a considerable discount.

B   How far could you go?

S   Myself? I think with the price that we have already I could not go beyond 2½ per cent at this stage. That would be my absolute limit.

B   And how far could your company go at the next stage?

S   When I say at this stage, I mean that with this particular deal 2½ per cent would be as far as we could go as a company.

Notes

quotation on spot by reminding him that competitors have quoted keener prices.

Salesman resists.

Buyer squeezes him.

Buyer presses to test if salesman's limit and his company's has *really* been reached.

B That's the limit?

S That would be the limit,
yes.

B So you're saying that the   Buyer expresses doubt.
company limit and your
limit are the same?

S Yes, it would be, with
the concessions that we have
already made on delivery
and parts stock and so on,
and the price that we had
initially. I think that
would be as much of a
package as we would be
able to put together, and
indeed we only reached
that level being pretty sure
that this machine would
prove very attractive to
you and then would give
you the purchase price.

B I wouldn't want you to   Buyer raises the spectre
misunderstand me,   of lower competitive
Mr Edmunds. The package   quotations again.
that you are now quoting
to me is no better than
the package that I have
received from several of
your competitors.

S But if we were to go to   Salesman tries to close.
the extra 2½ per cent?
Would that make it into a
deal which would be
acceptable to you?

B It might be. I must confess   Buyer tries to undermine
I am a little bit surprised   the salesman's status.
that on the sort of
contracts you negotiate
your company doesn't give
you more authority in
this area.

S Well the authority does
   stretch a good deal further
   than 2½ per cent, but we
   already have discounted
   considerably on the
   quotation that you have.
   Indeed I am not sure that
   the 2½ per cent itself isn't
   a major concession. I am
   quite sure that we couldn't
   go further than that at this
   stage. The 2½ per cent
   would be as far as we
   would be able to go.

B Don't forget of course   Buyer uses the 'I help
   that although we are   you, why don't you help
   talking about the initial   me?' technique.
   purchase of ten machines
   I think you know only too
   well the rate of expansion
   that this company has
   enjoyed over the past few
   years, and I think it's
   also only fair to say to
   you that during that
   period you have had a
   larger slice of our initial
   plant purchases than you
   used to enjoy.

S Yes, indeed.

B Now that is the relationship that I personally
   would like to continue
   but of course I have
   responsibilities to the
   board. The other
   consideration is that the
   purchase of further
   machines of whatever type,
   as you well know, depends
   very much on which   Buyer paints the picture

machines we buy initially,   of a possible rosy
because if we are familiar   future.
with them, our customers
are familiar with them,
and so on. Now, that being
the case, and I think we
have come to a reasonable
arrangement on the other
areas, is there anything   Tries again for a larger
you can do about that   price reduction.
2½ per cent?

S   Quite honestly, Mr Johnson,   Salesman refuses.
    if I were able to take it
    further than that I would.
    I am willing to take it
    back to my company, but
    I think it exceptionally
    unlikely that they would
    make any change. Indeed
    I am going to get my
    fingers caned quite hard
    for going so far as I have,
    but 2½ per cent would be
    as far as I would be
    willing to go.

B   Well I'll tell you what I
    will do. 2½ per cent is
    within your authority?

S   Yes, it is.

B   Let's make sure we have   Buyer summarises revised
    got these points right.   terms:
    You will take back from us
    after twelve months, if   *Parts stock.*
    we have not used them, the
    Class 'C' spares at no
    cost to ourselves.

S   Yes, we will.

B   You will paint these ten   *Livery.*
    machines and any
    subsequent machines that
    we may buy from you in

our new livery prior to
delivery?

S Yes, of course.

B As far as delivery is   *Delivery.*
   concerned, we are talking
   about ten machines, three
   to London, three to
   Birmingham, two to
   Manchester and one to
   Glasgow, one to
   Plymouth, free of charge.

S Yes, yes indeed.

B You're going to train   *Training.*
   between twenty to twenty-
   five people on our
   premises and all you need
   to do is to lay on the
   trainer and the machine to
   carry out the training
   programme.

S Yes.

B And as far as the initial   *Price.*
   purchase is concerned you
   will reduce that quoted
   price by 2½ per cent.

S Yes.

B Well, I think on that   *Buyer closes.*
   basis, Mr Edmunds, if you
   can sign up this morning I
   am prepared to place this
   initial order with you.

S Well, that's fine. I am very
   grateful. I am sure that
   that will go very well
   indeed.

B Good. Now you will
   confirm this to me in
   writing.

S Yes I will. I'll do that
   today, as soon as I get
   back to the office.

B I'll get your letter
tomorrow?

S Yes, yes you will.

B On receipt of your letter
confirming these points I
will then send you the
purchase order. Would
you like it to be addressed
to you personally at your
head office?

S Please, if you would. Yes.

B Well, thank you very
much.

S I hope you'll be very
pleased with it.

B I hope so. You will hear
from me if we are not.

S Thank you very much, Mr
Johnson.

B Thank you. Goodbye.

Table 5.1
Negotiation principles: check-list

Principle	Comments
1 Negotiation is the act or process of bargaining to reach a mutually acceptable agreement or objective.	Both sides must feel they have won, but not regret what the other side has achieved because it is not seen as gained at his expense. Each side achieves what it feels is most important.
2 Negotiation must take place between equals – in each other's eyes.	Although titles may be different, the ability of either side to make matching decisions is essential as is the mutual respect between negotiators that both count as equals.

Table 5.1 (continued)

Principle	Comments
3 Negotiation is based on a common respect for the rules of the game.	Be yourself. Discuss rather than debate. Neither side must attempt 'one-up-manship'. At the same time neither side yields anything that is really important to him, although he may well indicate the opposite. Avoid domination.
4 Put your cards on the table.	Don't pretend negotiating powers you do not possess. Declare what you can do and what you cannot do.
5 Be patient.	In negotiation rushed decisions are rarely good ones that satisfy either side. Be prepared to take time and don't hurry. Delay is better than a bad decision.
6 See the other side's case – unemotionally.	Often called empathy, being able to put yourself in the negotiating position of the person opposite you without being blinkered or emotionally involved helps your assessment of his position.
7 Communicate to advance relationship and negotiation objectives.	Be open and disclose your motives and self interest. Lay it on the line and let the buyer do so in turn. Don't be obscure.
8 Avoid confrontation.	Don't put yourself in a position from which you cannot retract. If you have

Table   5.1 (continued)

Principle	Comments
	a row things are said which can make negotiating impossible. Avoid showdowns. Stand firm but always state your position calmly.
9 If you disagree do so as from a devil's advocate position.	Be prepared to disagree by looking at your case from the buyer's point of view. This enables you to say things that do not confront the buyer nor gives rise to a confrontation.
10 Give a bit at a time.	Never concede everything or nothing. Give slice by slice, but for every concession you give get one back: 'If you do this I will do that'.
11 Know when to leave well alone.	In negotiation there is rarely an ideal solution, so don't pursue one when it is beyond your reach, too costly or takes more time than you can afford.
12 Declare company strategies if you must, but not objectives behind them.	Company strategies and plans become public knowledge as soon as they are implemented, but the objectives, personal motivations and needs that give them birth, impetus and fuel them should be kept secret.
13 Don't compromise your ultimate objectives.	Set your highest and lowest negotiating objective, then don't settle below the lowest point. Lose rather than gain a worthless deal.

Table   5.1 (continued)

Principle	Comments
14 Never relax your guard.	Stamina is one of the hallmarks of a good negotiator. Your opponent may stall for hours just to find out when you will crack. If you can't bide your time in such duels don't negotiate.
15 Always rehearse your case.	Tell yourself what you are going to say, how you are going to say it and when. Then rehearse how your opposite numbers will do the same.
16 Don't underestimate other people.	Many negotiators pretend not to know or to be foolish. Some are fools, but others may appear so to mislead you.
17 Respect confidences given in negotiating.	Don't ever betray a confidence learnt during negotiation. The essence of negotiation is mutual trust.
18 End negotiations positively.	Satisfactory negotiations should end when both sides can part without regret. Try to end all negotiations on a positive basis of satisfying the needs of all parties.

6 Buyer behaviour

The traditionally trained salesman has some fairly clearly defined objectives: to identify the needs of customers within the limits of those his products or services can meet and satisfy, and then to persuade a sufficient number of people to buy to enable him to meet or exceed his sales target. His two weapons are the *products* he sells and his *persuasive skills*. The salesman, on balance, will tend to succeed more often than not if the *product inspires confidence* in the purchaser or user by living up to or exceeding the promises or claims made about it. That confidence once established, repeat sales can be expected just so long as the product performance remains good or exceeds expectations. Problems will undoubtedly arise if there are technical failures, administrative muddles over the customer's account, or when a competitor comes along with an identical product at a cheaper price or offers one that is better. Nevertheless the two essential elements are confidence in the product and the persuasive skills of the salesman.

But in negotiation the starting point is not confidence in the product because product and service performance are for the most part no longer in question. They are accepted. And so confidence shifts from product performance to the salesman.

The very essence of negotiation is that it is concerned with *profit* and all that influences profit. Therefore the *negotiating salesman must inspire confidence* in those with whom he negotiates that he understands the customer's profit needs, the mechanisms that influence profit and that he can communicate and negotiate about such matters and establish confidence in the different levels of people he deals with in customer companies. The product salesman who directs his selling towards groups of buyers with common needs will be tempted to treat customers as though their behaviour patterns were the same.

The negotiator's relationship with buyers is not just a persuasive one. Indeed he must, if he is to succeed, change the buyer's perception of him from being a persuader to being a problem solver, a profit improver. He must be perceived as being positively related to making profits – for the buyer.

Different levels of negotiating relationships

This perception must be shared by more than one person in the customer organisation. Rarely are negotiated decisions the result of dealing with one person. So the negotiator must be able to deal with and relate to:

1 Different levels of personnel, from directors to operatives.
2 Different groups of decision makers; some will be generalists, others will be specialists concerned with technical part-decisions.
3 Different disciplines; marketing men, financial experts, engineers, production, personnel.
4 Different backgrounds and motivations.

The negotiating salesman not only moves between these different groups, but also has to understand the factors that influence their behaviour patterns and how these affect his relationships with them. Since these behaviour patterns alternate between official roles and personal roles, the salesman must be sensitive to and understand deeply but not censoriously. In particular he must identify in each key customer organisation:

1 Company personality and philosophy.
2 Company's management or leadership style.
3 Personality and needs of buyers involved in negotiation.

Company personality and philosophy

Commercial organisations are made up of groups of people who work together to achieve a variety of objectives, of which the need to survive and/or to prosper will depend upon those in whose hands power lies. Like salesmen, customer companies seek to satisfy their needs. For some this may be survival, or the avoidance of failure, whilst for others it is the constant search for success, the need to be top in everything, to achieve.

A. H. Maslow's *Theory of Human Motivation* gives us a valuable insight into what stimulates human behaviour towards certain goals, and provides clues to a company's as well as to an individual's behaviour. He suggests that man's needs are organised in the form of a pyramid or hierarchy (see Figure 6.1). At the most basic level our needs are those essential to sustain life – our physiological needs for such things as food, shelter, water, clothing. At the next level, once these basic needs are satisfied, come our safety needs. The average person needs and prefers to have a safe, orderly, predictable and organised life and to reduce to the minimum the unpredictable, dangerous things. If both the physiological and safety needs are being satisfied then man turns to the need to belong, to love and be loved and to have a recognised place in a group. At its most basic as a member of a family, in the larger context in the social community within which the family lives and then in the work group. The satisfaction of this need to belong, established, gives rise to another need – the need for respect, for self-esteem, for the esteem of others, for the satisfaction of one's ego.

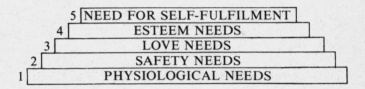

Figure 6.1   The hierarchy of needs

The satisfaction of these four sets of needs, on a continuous and fairly uninterrupted basis – the *physiological*, *safety*, *love*, and *esteem* needs – leads ultimately to discontent unless an individual is doing that which he really feels he is fitted for and wants to do as opposed necessarily to what he is doing.

These needs vary from person to person. Likewise in commercial terms they vary from company to company and the negotiating salesman should consider the needs of key account customers in terms of the following:

1   Is the company's profitability so low or non-existent that the dominant need is the basic one of survival, or is the chief executive hell bent on beating his only rival in the market, or obtaining the accolade of public recognition through a title or the Queen's Award for Industry?

2   Except in extreme circumstances the majority of customers' needs are a mixture to be satisfied ranging from improving security of a division's survival to gaining the approval of the local community, so that a favourable climate of opinion will sway the local authorities to grant permission for a factory extension or new office block.

3   A satisfied need is not a motivator. Whilst for all practical purposes every company has needs to be satisfied it is the degree and extent that the negotiator must be aware of.

4   The lower the level of customer need, the easier it is to satisfy. But most customers' needs tend to be at the higher levels which are more complex to understand and more difficult to satisfy.

The achievers and the failure avoiders

Companies can also be identified in their philosophy by whether they are actively and aggressively seeking to achieve larger profits, market dominance, be the first to invent a new product or process, or are merely trying to avoid failure. To some extent these two extremes mirror the age of the company and the drives of its directing executives.

Styles of leadership

The way in which a customer company reaches buying decisions usually reflects the style of management or leadership that exists. There are three main styles characterised by clearly recognisable differences:

1 *Autocracy or dictatorship*

Here the chief executive lays down the policy by telling everyone what he wants done. He is rarely receptive to people telling him what they think, and so when negotiating with companies where this style exists it is a waste of time dealing with intermediaries; you must deal with the principal. But you will also notice that in sub-groups in such a company, the leader in each one tends to exhibit a dictatorship style and this will be common throughout the organisation.

2 *Democratic*

At the opposite extreme to the autocratic dictatorship style is what is known as the democratic, committee or bottom-up style of management. In such a company, management puts all its decisions to groups at every level of decision-making. The groups arrive, by a process of majority choice, at decisions, usually the least risky of those open to them, and their choice becomes the management's decision. It is always pleasant dealing with such companies. The staff are friendly and not threatening, the management open and usually approachable. But from a negotiating angle, decisions tend to be long-drawn-out and conservative in character. Innovation and taking calculated risks are seldom the characteristics found in companies managed over-democratically.

3 *Participative or benevolent autocracy*

This style is where senior management is usually decisive but seeks the positive participation of its staff in the decisions that are reached.

Management asks staff for its views and comments on key decisions and in the light of these comments decides upon a course of action which may reflect some, all or none of the ideas that have been fed to it. But the act of consultation provides a positive environment wherein there tend to be creativity and the taking of calculated risks; ideas are explored and innovative approaches are encouraged.

The organisation's profile

All these factors contribute to the profile of a customer organisation in terms of the climate in which its people work, the way decisions are made, the urgency and tempo of work, how people communicate with one another; the way power is distributed and the amount of it that is delegated and to whom; the characteristics and personalities of the key personnel with whom you have to negotiate and the roles people play in the various groups in which you meet them.

Buying decision groups

Negotiating is a complex art and, because of the far-reaching implications of major negotiations, many people are concerned in a customer company and contribute to the final decision. For these reasons, you must not only know what groups are involved in reaching negotiated decisions but equally who else, either individually or as groups, influence buying decisions. You need to identify:

1   What are the decision-making groups and the levels of decisions they reach?
2   What are the specialist/expert groups who influence the major decision-making groups?
3   Who are the leaders in each group?
4   Who are the members of each group?
5   What types of decision does each group make and take?
6   What are the behaviour patterns of each group? For example, does a product planning group always meet at a certain time before the buying committee meets with suppliers, etc.?

Where does power reside?

At a certain negotiation meeting the leader of one side of the negotiations became so incensed by the apparent inability of the other side to come to a decision that he spat out the question: 'Am I dealing with the engine driver or the oil rag?' *Negotiation can only succeed between equals with equal power to reach a mutually acceptable decision.*

If one side or the other does not possess such power then inevitably the negotiations break down. So it is essential to understand the distribution of power in its various forms in key customer companies and to have an up-to-date intelligence of the coming generation of power-holders. You should know:

1 *Power of position:*
Do the people with grand-sounding titles always have the power to match them? Titles are too often exchanged for power!

2 *Power behind the throne:*
   (a)   Who are the people whose opinion is always asked before major decisions are reached?
   (b)   Who influences the decision-makers?
   (c)   Whose opinions help to frame policy?

3 *Power of expert:*
   (a)   Some decisions are made by experts behind the scenes and the decision-makers just pass on what the experts say.
   (b)   Some decisions are never reached without clearance by the experts.
   (c)   Who are these experts and what is the source or basis of their power? Frequently it resides with the financial adviser or director.

Power is not an easy thing to define or to perceive. If it is held by one person then there is precious little for anyone else to exercise. But because it tends to be distributed in different ways in different companies, look for clues that provide the answers to four questions:

1   Who has the power to compel others to do things?
2   Who has the power to influence or decide what is done?
3   Who has the limited power in certain circumstances to influence?
4   Who has expert power?

A check-list has been constructed (Table 6.1), to help you to analyse customer organisation profiles, behaviour patterns and motivations, and power.

Table 6.1
Customer organisation profiles: check-list

	Yes	No	Notes
Management style			
Autocracy–Dictatorship			
Democratic			
Participative			
Irrational			
Decision-making process			
One-man			
Committee/bottom-up			
Consultative			
Specialist			
Company character			
Aggressive			
Conservative			
Creative			
Risk-taking			
Traditional			
Communication system			
Free and open			
Friendly			
Formal			
Guarded–defensive			
Bureaucratic			
Image–personality			
Achievers			
Failure avoiders			
Inventive/innovative			
Imitators			
Co-operative			
Success–seeking			

Other factors

7   The buyer's role

You will be aware from your own experience and from the previous chapter on buyer behaviour of the importance of the buyer's attitude, not only of the objective view he has of his company's needs, but his own needs, likes and dislikes. Rarely do any of us in business make buying decisions which are either completely objective and rational or wholly emotional. The buyers of capital items and industrial goods are influenced in their decisions by such things as prestige and security, whilst at the other end of the scale people buying food will be influenced by objective factors such as price and value as well as the appeals to the palate. Diagrammatically this mixture of buying motives is illustrated in Figure 7.1.

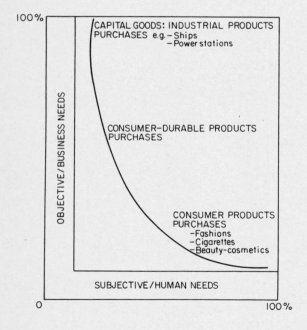

Figure 7.1   Objective and subjective buying influences. At neither extreme does graph of needs actually touch axis showing that all buying decisions are based on a mixture of objective and subjective needs.

Even though objectivity is usually greater when a person is buying an industrial product for his company, the importance of his personal needs is revealed and confirmed by such observations made by salesmen as: 'He does business with me because we get on so well.' 'Our sort of selling is long term, where you build up a relationship.' 'You've got to sell yourself.' This personal contact is critical in negotiation, but it does have dangers. When we know someone well we can easily take our relationship for granted. The signs we look for when making an initial contact with a person can be ignored once we know them. Yet in negotiation they are critical.

Buyer/salesman interaction

Everything we do or say when we are with a buyer causes a reaction on his part. Everything he does or says causes a reaction on our part. Every salesman is aware of this and is careful to conduct a discussion in a logical sequence. In this way he can lead the buyer through a presentation step by step, to the ultimate of the final action, agreement.

Interaction in negotiation

Once there is agreement that the buyer does have long-term need of your products, the importance of this interaction does not cease. It increases. In times of 'normal' supply the danger lies in relaxing your guard once the buyer has agreed to take the product. A skilled buyer can gain for himself a number of valuable concessions from a salesman who misinterprets the former's reaction as one of having agreed *all the conditions* of sale. By negotiation the buyer takes the necessary initiative to optimise his position in any given purchase. Without negotiation, he is merely accepting the best offer given him.

What are the buyer's objectives?

Once agreement has been reached in principle about the supply of a product or service, a buyer's aim is to gain as many advantages for his company as he can. His strength in achieving these will be affected by how much competition there is in the field, how good a price analysis he has made; how much business he has to offer the supplier; and how much time is available to reach an agreement. At the same time he will seek to establish your bargaining strength – how much you want/need the business; how anxious you are to establish yourself with his company and what concessions you may be willing to make to achieve this end. A buyer who has developed an alternate supplier goes into the negotiation in a strong position.

What are the buyer's tactics?

Discussions with a buyer will follow several stages.

Salesman

Persuading the buyer to accept a price rise or a delivery schedule by showing benefits. Answers questions. Finds way round objections.

The salesman must be watching for this danger. Spotting the exact moment when the buyer has accepted the idea in principle is critical.

The salesman now needs to discuss the exact terms and conditions. (Preparation will help greatly to define exactly

Buyer

Questions/raises objections.

The skilled buyer will prolong this stage because many salesmen will be tempted to concede many points in an attempt to overcome apparent objections.

This may be in a number of ways:
(a) a change in the type of question;
(b) increased attention;
(c) picking up a sample specification;
(d) changing the subject;
(e) becoming more questioning;
(f) becoming less questioning;
(g) becoming more aggressive;
(h) becoming less aggressive;
(i) relaxing.

what he wants to achieve, and hopefully the areas of interest to the buyer.)

The buyer will be playing down the real value to himself of points offered by the salesman and the value of points he wants to gain for himself.

Agreement is needed on each point.

Some buyers will suddenly switch to apparent objections to try to weaken a salesman.

The skilled salesman ignores it as an objection, but handles it by looking for a balancing concession.

Emphasises the objection and plays down the concession.

Agreement is reached when the *perceived* value to each side is seen to be fair.

Whilst some people criticise or dismiss this 'game', it can have considerable impact on the value of an order to both the customer and you.

Conclusion

In negotiation, the importance of watching a buyer's reactions and judging where he is in the sequence of the discussion increases with the length of time you have known the customer. Both the short- and long-term profitability of the supplier can be maintained or improved by your skill in this area.

8   Planning the negotiation

Negotiation is a role which should be planned with professional care and which involves the co-ordination of every level of marketing and sales activity. The professional success of your negotiations will be influenced by the extent and quality of your planning and preparation. The financial implications of negotiation are considerable. Your planning needs to span three key areas to ensure both your volume and profit goals are achieved.

1   The development of a company strategy.
2   Customer/account planning.
3   Negotiation control.

The development of a company strategy

You should ask yourself major questions about markets, company and competition.

Markets

1   What proportion of existing and prospective customers expect to negotiate all the conditions of purchase, i.e. including those other than price?
2   What proportion of different categories of customer expect to negotiate?
3   What percentage of present sales volume do they represent?
4   What percentage of present profits is produced by sales to these customers?
5   What proportion of cases involves:

   (a) a group decision?
   (b) a decision made by one man alone or with the advice of others?
   (c) informed professional purchasing?
   (d) first-time purchase/re-purchase?
   (e) government bodies in decision-making?

6   How strong are the buyers; what is the strength of their need to buy relative to your need to sell?

7   What proportion of negotiations involve contractual agreements? Do they include non-price factors?

8   How can a planned and skilled negotiation strategy help to service the market?

Company

1   What are the company's commercial and marketing objectives?

2   How does existing negotiated business aid or conflict with these?

3   What strengths and weaknesses are highlighted?

4   Are any changes necessary in the ways in which you negotiate business? For example, looking at past cases honestly: on which sides of the points of need balance did you conclude business?

5   Who is currently responsible for selling to whom at what levels? For example: Is too much or too little responsibility being given/taken? Should greater responsibility for price/discount negotiation be given to salesmen? Does the level of contact meet the real needs of the market?

6   What levels of negotiating skills and authority are needed – and what levels exist?

7   What commercial and marketing benefits could result from better negotiation, or from applying negotiation skills to a wider level of sales activities? For example: Are you really satisfied with present margins from negotiated business? Are you really sure that you are obtaining the optimum share of volume from some industries?

8   How can a planned and skilled negotiation strategy help the company?

Competition

1   Do you know how well your competitors perform in negotiating business?

2   What are their apparent strengths and weaknesses in negotiation? Look, for example, at speed of decision: range of authority (particularly in respect of price and delivery); product range – service; distribution – capacity:cost:volume.

3   To what extent do they appear to strengthen or weaken the market?

4 What relationship can be perceived between the answer to 3 and correlation of their volume to their profitability?
5 What are their main concessions?
6 How do your plans compare with theirs?
7 How can you minimise their impact when you are negotiating with the buyer?
8 How can a planned and skilled negotiation strategy help to beat the competition?

Customer/account planning

In any successful negotiation – whether it is a major account strategy or one individual interview – you are concerned with three key elements.

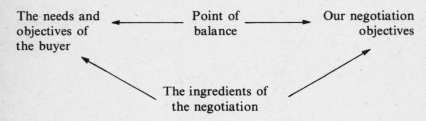

You need, therefore, to approach customer/account negotiation planning in six stages:

1 Assess the objective and subjective needs of the buyer.
2 From these identify the major areas for negotiation.
3 Relate the costs and value (both real and perceived) of concessions on both sides in each major area.
4 Assess both the actual stances likely to be adopted by the buyer and the stated stances with which he will open the negotiation.
5 Relate these to the commercial and marketing objectives you have set.
6 Decide your own actual and opening stances relative to the buyer's and plan your conduct of the interview.

Negotiation planning: Assessing the needs

Taking each in turn, the answers to a systematic question check-list will provide the information we need to have for efficient customer/account negotiation planning:

1   *What are the customer's marketing policies?*

For example:

    1   Which markets does he operate in?
    2   What methods of distribution of his products does he favour (i.e. selling to wholesalers, or to retailers)?
    3   Does he use agents?

2   *What are his major marketing strategies?*

For example:

    1   Which market segments does he concentrate on?
    2   Against which of his products does he concentrate marketing and promotional support?
    3   Against which distribution outlets does he concentrate marketing effort?
    4   How does he position his company products in the market?
    5   Is he new-product orientated?
    6   What are his new-product development priorities?
    7   What is his pricing policy?
    8   What priority does he give to exports?
    9   What are the geographical limits of his distribution activities?

3   *What marketing tactics does he use?*

For example:

    1   Is he keen on promotion?
    2   Is he advertising-orientated?
    3   What is the level of professionalism of his salesmen/sales staff?
    4   Does he promote new products effectively?
    5   Does he use marketing techniques to maximum advantage to sell his products to the ultimate consumer?
    6   Does he like incentives for himself?

4   *What sort of customers does he have?*

For example:

    1   Are they wholesalers, retailers, or ultimate consumers/end users?
    2   Are his trade customers the most efficient/progressive in the market?

3   To what age/class/income groups do his ultimate consumers belong?

5   *What are the trends in his market?*

   1   How are his markets affected by economic conditions, both locally and worldwide?
   2   How is his business affected by his competitors?
   3   What warehouse space does he really have available for your products?
   4   Which competitors does he favour or have a grudge against?

6   *What are the commercial n·eds of the buyer?*

   1   In what way does the purchase or non-purchase of your product affect his business?
   2   What problems does he have?
   3   What alternatives are open to him?
   4   What are his subjective needs?
   5   How important are they?

7   *The major ingredients of negotiation*

   1   What is important to the buyer in making his decision?
   2   In what areas will he seek to negotiate most keenly?
   3   What combination of, for example, cost, price, volume, technical support, delivery terms, credit, availability, stock holding, training?
   4   Exclusive terms – specification.
   5   After-sales service.
   6   Extended guarantees.

8   *Costs and value of concessions*

   1   What concessions does/can the buyer offer?
   2   What will he expect in exchange?
   3   What will be the cost to both sides relative to the returns in each area?
   4   What concessions which·cost you little will be of considerable value to the buyer?
   5   Which concessions are most expensive?
   6   Within what range are you each likely to operate?

(See Table 8.1.)

Table 8.1
Check-list of possible concessions

Concessions from customer	Concessions from seller
Storage rate	Special facilities (e.g. heating)
Use of cost index and date	Storage rate
Break points	Standard of service
Labelling of cases	Frequency of service
Palletisation	Ancillary services (price marking)
Drop size and minimum	Documentation
Carton size and shape	Special vehicle facilities (tail lifts)
Delivery frequency	Vehicle access priority
Stacking requirements	Management information
Stock turn-round	Containerisation
Delivery priority	Order processing
Number of lines	Office accommodation
Delivery points	Payment terms
Increased through-put	Breaking bulk
Forecasting	Order progressing
Prompt payment	Shrink wrapping
	Labelling

9   *Assess the buyer's stances*

1   What is the real strength of the buyer's need?
2   How will he *state* the strength of his need by his opening stance?
3   What means will he use to pull you towards this position?
4   What is your estimate of the actual stance the buyer will take after negotiation?

10   *Relate these to your own objectives*

1   What do you need to achieve?
2   In what ways do the buyer's needs match or conflict with your own objectives?
3   Can any major differences be resolved by negotiation?

11   *Decide your stances and plan the conduct of negotiation*

1   What bargaining points do you have?
2   How can the value of these to the buyer be raised relative to the cost to you?

3   What concessions can be expected from the buyer and how do these match your bargaining points?
4   Where should the negotiation take place?
5   Who should be involved?
6   Should points be dealt with individually or as a 'package'?
7   How can the meeting be planned to give you opportunity to seek agreement at each stage?

Negotiation control

However well you set out objectives, no matter how soundly based your strategies, you will fail if you do not exercise careful control. Failure to do so can so easily result in a 'corporate give-away' which in the long term benefits no one.

The ingredients of any negotiation have a value and a cost to both sides of the negotiation. In planning and controlling your negotiation activity you are concerned with balancing the needs of your customers with those of your company and with ensuring that as a result both benefit.

It is essential, therefore, for you to recognise the nature of the costs of each ingredient to you (and to control them carefully) whilst at the same time planning on the basis of the ingredients which are important to the customer and relative values which he attaches to them.

Controlling costs in planning

All the ingredients of the negotiation represent a potential cost to you in the form of concessions. *You should therefore know what these costs are,* for example:

1   What is the *cost* of a price concession?
2   What is the *cost* of providing technical and financial services?
3   What is the *cost* of a delivery concession?
4   What is the *cost* of making unique products for customers?
5   What is the *cost* of offering design facilities?
6   What is the *cost* of your advisory/after-sales services?
7   What is the *cost* of extended credit?
8   What is the *cost* of over-selling volume and having to meet a deadline with overtime?
9   What is the *cost* of holding stocks for customers in your warehouses?
10   What is the *cost* of making any promise?

You should not just concern yourself exclusively with costs – you must relate these costs to the value which they may attract in terms of volume and profits. But if as negotiators you have inadequate knowledge or perception of costs, and exercise slipshod control over your use of concessions, you can erode profitability without in any way adding to the value which customers place on your products or services – in fact you are as likely to depreciate their value in the customers' eyes. Ultimately a stage can be reached where the costing systems and budgetary controls which you use take account of these factors and should be built into your negotiation planning. It is then that:

1 Any negotiator with *authority* to give a concession can also be held *accountable* for its cost.

2 Concessions given can be shown as a cost in performance summaries relating to volume and revenue. If actual costs cannot be assessed then notional ones can be considered and agreed.

3 Concessional costs can be budgeted and allocated to each negotiator and/or major account plan.

4 Budgetary control can give appropriate responsibility and authority, but should prevent any negotiator giving concessions whose cost will be borne elsewhere, for example the extra cost of overtime working.

5 Actual costs have more impact than percentage figures. Budgetary control summaries should show percentage concessions in money terms.

6 Even if concessionary budgets allow discretion across a range of accounts then limits should be agreed to avoid the problems of gross anomalies.

Some examples

The following examples of four different types of business illustrate the degree of preparation that can be done before entering into negotiations with buyers:

1 *Agriculture:* Acquisition/disposal of pastoral property (Table 8.2).

2 *Food/Livestock:* Purchase of grain/livestock (Table 8.3).

3 *Meat:* Lease of abattoirs and/or boning room (Table 8.4).

4 *Meat products:* Sale of meat products (Table 8.5).

Table 8.2

Acquisition/disposal of pastoral property

Main negotiating points	Buyer's view	Seller's view	Concessions given		Concessions obtained	
			Type	Amount	Type	Amount
1 What is included in vendor's price (a) property bare (normally would include all buildings, fences, and plant being integral to building, i.e. shearing plant, lighting plant); (b) farm plant, in or out of sale; (c) livestock, in or out of sale; (d) stores, in or out of sale; (e) fodder and						

Main negotiating points	Buyer's view	Seller's view	Concessions given		Concessions obtained	
			Type	Amount	Type	Amount
fertiliser stocks, in or out of sale; (f) growing crops; or (g) walk-in-walk out.						
2 Where consumable items included, the delivery quantities.						
3 Price for 1, above.						
4 Allocation of purchase price in contract.	Buyer wants market value or higher for depreciable assets, livestock and other items to obtain tax advantages.	Seller wants tax written down values or less to obtain tax advantages.				
5 Who has right to harvest growing crops, if any.	Buyer may want crop to offset some of purchase price.	Seller may want growing crop for cash-flow purposes.				
6 Vacant possession.	Buyer may wish to obtain possession before settlement to (a) avoid agist-	Seller may not wish to give possession to avoid performance of contract without				

Table 8.2 (continued)

Main negotiating points	Buyer's view	Seller's view	Concessions given		Concessions obtained	
			Type	Amount	Type	Amount
	ment; (b) have somewhere to live; (c) harvest growing crop for which he may offer a rental pending settlement.	payment of purchase price or may find it convenient to give possession to avoid paying carrying on expenditure.				
7 Settlement, time, place, method, i.e. cash, bank cheque, terms on satisfactory security.	Buyer may want settlement, say after 31st December, to avoid land tax on land held at that date. Buyer may want short- or long-term finance of balance of purchase money.	Seller may want settlement prior to 31st December to avoid liability for land tax. Seller may want cash or accept terms to provide income from an investment or as a means of selling rather than hold out for cash buyer.				
8 Adjustments clause for differences between actual and contracted del-	Buyer would want some protection and compensation for deliveries less	Vendor may not wish to receive less for stores, fodder and other consumables				

Main negotiating points	Buyer's view	Seller's view	Concessions given		Concessions obtained	
			Type	Amount	Type	Amount
iveries of live-stock, plant, stores and fodder in 1, above.	than quantities contracted.	used in maintaining stock and crops from date of contract to date of settlement.				
9 Easements and encroachments and minor tenure matters.	Buyer may want some reduction of pur-chase price for give-and-take fence lines, neighbour's irrigation channels traversing property.	Vendor wants buyer to accept give-and-take arrangements for fencing, ease-ments and encroach-ments.				
10 Employee's accom-modation meeting requirements of Rural Workers' Accommodation Act.	Buyer may require an indemnity as to costs of complying with Act.	Vendor may wish to sell on an 'as is' basis with the buyer to satisfy himself on compliance with the Act.				
11 Liability to con-tinuing employees for annual, sick, long-service, and other leave.	Buyer does not accept liability without indemnity or adjust-ment on settlement.	Vendor wishes to terminate employees' services rather than pay purchaser the liability.				
12 Other conditions and warranties.						

Table 8.3
Purchase of grain/livestock

Main negotiating points	Buyer's view	Seller's view	Concessions given		Concessions obtained	
			Type	Value	Type	Value
1 Description, quantity and other specification. Is sale based on sale by sample description or buyer's inspection?	Full description and specification to be in writing.	Sale as inspected. Caveat emptor applies.				
2 Price.						
3 Delivery: time, place, to whom.	Delivery at buyer's premises within two weeks of acceptance.	Delivery at seller's premises on acceptance.				
4 At whose risk pending delivery?	Vendor's risk until delivery.	Purchaser's risk on acceptance.				
5 Right of rejection: (a) inferior to sample;	Has rights under Sale of Goods Act. Usual for buyer	Inspection 'as is' without right of rejection and				

Main negotiating points	Buyer's view	Seller's view	Concessions given		Concessions obtained	
			Type	Amount	Type	Amount
(b) blind, lame and diseased.	to reject lame, blind and diseased livestock.	caveat emptor applies.				
6 Payment: time, place, method (i.e. cash or terms).	Half purchase price on delivery, balance within one month.	Cash on acceptance.				
7 Other conditions and warranty.						

121

Table 8.4
Lease of abattoirs and/or boning room

Main negotiating points	Lessor's view	Lessee's view	Concessions given		Concessions obtained	
			Type	Amount	Type	Amount
1 Description, area and other details of buildings, plant and facilities to be the subject of a lease.	Lessor wants to provide all facilities for exclusive use by lessee.	Lessee wants to lease all facilities for his exclusive use.				
2 Engagement and cost of labour where labour facilities being hired: (a) slaughter-men, boners, etc.; (b) supervisors; (c) Management.	Lessor to provide all labour, supervisory staff and management.	Lessee wants to use own labour.				
3 Who is entitled to by-products?	Negotiate with 7, below.	Lessee entitled.				
4 Who is to control operations?	Lessor controls operations.	Lessee to control.				

Main negotiating points	Lessor's view	Lessee's view	Concessions given		Concessions obtained	
			Type	Amount	Type	Amount
5 What rental concessions are to be given for breakdowns of machinery, and interruptions (perhaps industrial)? Is there any abatement of rental in event of close-down for any reason or certain reasons?	Lessor wants no abatement.	Lessee wants abatement of rental for all lost time through circumstances beyond his control.				
6 Consideration for the granting of the lease. Consider: high rental and low cost per head of through-put; low rental and high cost per head of through-put.	Lessor wants high minimum rental and not concerned with through-put to cover overhead.	Lessee wants low rental but fixed cost per head to facilitate costing procedures.				

123

Table 8.4 (continued)

Main negotiating points	Lessor's view	Lessee's view	Concessions given		Concessions obtained	
			Type	Amount	Type	Amount
7 Term of lease.	5 years.	2 years.				
8 Options, if any, on termination of lease.	No options.	Option to purchase at fixed figure or renewal of lease for further two years.				
9 Capital expenditure. Who pays? Where incurred by reason of compliance with statutory requirements and licensing authorities. Consider:	At lessee's expense.					
(a) percentage per annum of cost;		10 per cent per annum of cost provided maximum rental, not in excess of additional $5,000 p.a.				
(b) if more than, say, $20,000, cost is to be paid by lessor; if less than, say $20,000, cost is to be paid by lessee.						

Table 8.5
Sale of meat products

Main negotiating points	Buyer's view	Seller's view	Concessions given		Concessions obtained	
			Type	Amount	Type	Amount
1 Typical costing of selling price bases on kill, bone and export CIF.						
Live animal cost 20c per lb						
Freight to abattoirs 1c per lb						
Raw material cost 21c per lb						
Killing costs 4c per lb						
Handling to distribution 2c per lb						
Boning 5c per lb						
Packing and wrapping 1c per lb						
Freezing 2c per lb						
35						

Table 8.5 (continued)

Main negotiating points	Buyer's view	Seller's view	Concessions given		Concessions obtained	
			Type	Amount	Type	Amount
70% yield (saleable products) say 50c per lb						
Overhead:						
Rent, supervisors, insurance, telephone, electricity: 8 cents						
Fixed 6c per lb						
Variable 2c per lb						
Charges to wharf and load on ship						
Freight } Wharf over-time 2c per lb						
FOB cost 60c per lb		Wants to sell at 62.5c FOB. Consider: higher through-put should over-absorb fixed cost and benefits				
CIF: Insurance and freight 9c per lb						
CIF cost 69c per lb						

Main negotiating points	Buyer's view	Seller's view	Concessions given		Concessions obtained	
			Type	Amount	Type	Amount
Profit margin 2c per lb / Selling price 71c per lb / Based on through-put 4,000 animals per month	Too dear – offers 70 cents CIF.	of economies of scale; lower through-put should under-absorb fixed overhead and perhaps strain recovery semi-variable costs.				
2 Delivery: timing.	Commence delivery within two months.	Commence delivery 90 days.				
3 Right of rejection.	Not equal to sample or specification.	At least equal to sample or specification.				
4 Settlement.	Cash on delivery at destination port, in buyer's currency.	Cash on production of shipping documents in seller's currency.				
5 Quantity.	Minimum 500 tonnes per month.	Minimum 650 tonnes per month.				
6 Duration of contract.	Four months.	Six months.				

Table 8.6
Illustration of costing control

Gross margin of target deal		
20% of £1000	200	
Less:		
1 *Cash conceded*		
Price discount of 2½%		25
Over-riding discount 1½%		15
Advertising support		20
		60
Remainder	140	
Less:		
2 *Costed non-price concessions*		
Split delivery		5
Non-standard pack		20
Two weeks extra credit		5
Additional merchandising support		20
		50
Net gross margin on deal	90	
= 9% retained (11% given away)		

Table 8.7
Negotiation strategy check-list

Strategy	Comments
1 Have a total negotiating plan.	Always know what you are going to do. If you have to break off to get further instructions because you get stuck through lack of planning you weaken your bargaining strength.

Strategy	Comments
2 Sit where you can command meeting.	Always place yourself if you can where you can see, watch and hear everyone else at the meeting.
3 Keep numbers to the minimum.	The fewer the participants the sooner agreement can usually be reached.
4 Learn all the key facts.	Only when you possess *all* the facts do you know what you can give or concede and afford to.
5 Don't be afraid to make an opening concession.	One of the arts of negotiating is knowing how to open. Be ready to make an opening concession. Use a minor one to show flexibility or to achieve a major compromise from the other side.
6 Be specific.	Every point agreed should be agreed in *specific terms*, so that there is no re-opening of discussion when the final agreement is turned into a written contract for signature.
7 Promise only what you can do.	Long-term business relationships can only be built on mutually fulfilled promises. Don't promise something you cannot do. Never over-sell.

Table 8.8
Check-list for negotiation planning

	Questions	Answers	Planning implications
1	What are the customer's marketing policies?		
2	What are his major marketing strategies?		
3	What marketing tactics does he use?		
4	What sort of customers does he have?		
5	What are the trends in his market?		
6	What are the commercial needs of the buyer?		
7	The major negotiation ingredients are?		
8	What are the costs and value of concessions involved?		
9	How do you assess the buyer's stances?		
10	How do these relate to your own objectives?		
11	What should your stances be?		
12	How will you control the negotiation?		

9 Conduct of negotiations

As we have seen, successful negotiation entails planning, and the plan must be based on a coherent strategy. In this chapter we look at the process of negotiation itself and see how various tactics can be used to achieve desired results.

At the end of the chapter are descriptions of two actual commercial situations, with the relevant negotiating points analysed, by way of example, from the point of view of both buyer and seller in each case.

What are the major strategic elements of negotiation?

Actual stances

Given the underlying common needs, the strategy of negotiation is concerned with the actual and stated magnitude of those needs on both sides.

S ——————— NB ——————— B
Actual supplier stance   ↑   Actual buyer stance
Point of need balance

At the start of a negotiation there will normally be a gap between the terms and conditions the buyer says he wants and what the supplier says he is prepared to offer. The major strategic task of the sales negotiator, whether the subject under negotiation is price or a non-price factor such as delivery, is to judge accurately the *actual* gap that exists between the parties, as opposed to the *stated* gap. The major initial strategic ploy in negotiations is for both sides to *exaggerate* the distance between them.

Initial stances

Sometimes (not always) a buyer will open up a negotiation by deliberately (or automatically) exaggerating his stance: 'Before we start, if you think I'm going to accept that price increase that came through the post the other day, forget it. It's high time somebody took a stand against this constant pushing up of prices.' Or he may attempt to suggest that he is not likely to come to an agreement because of other negative factors which he raises at the beginning of the interview.

If (as is often the case) this is a strategic ploy, he will, if you allow him to save face while doing so, move from his initial stance to an actual stance quite quickly and with little encouragement: 'Alright, let's talk about prices, but I warn you, you'll have to think very hard about that 10 per cent increase.'

You must be clear about the reasons for initial stance. It is done purely to disconcert the salesman. This can be seen clearly in an example of a trade union/management pay negotiation, where the opening stance comes from the trade union.

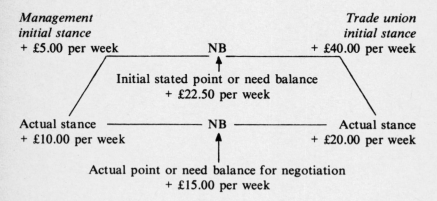

Management initial stance
+ £5.00 per week

NB

Trade union initial stance
+ £40.00 per week

Initial stated point or need balance
+ £22.50 per week

Actual stance ———————— NB ——————— Actual stance
+ £10.00 per week   + £20.00 per week

Actual point or need balance for negotiation
+ £15.00 per week

Thus, the first task is to establish by discussion the *actual* gap which exists between yourself and the buyer. This is invariably achieved by a mutual examination of the needs and covering benefits on both sides, but you must ensure that you limit the loss of position that this manoeuvring entails for both parties. Commonly the parties will take up their actual stances with ritualistic face-saving comments, which are important if the fabric of the negotiation is to be preserved. The negotiation then moves into its tactical stage.

Tactics of negotiation

You are now concerned with reaching, from the actual points of difference between the parties, a mutually acceptable agreement. You can see at this stage that the essence of negotiation is *compromise*, actual or apparent. The discussion now proceeds in a highly structured way, each side reducing the gap by a series of mutual *concessions*. At this stage the skilful negotiator *trades a concession*, which in fact costs him little, but which has a real or implied high value to the other party, and brings a relatively more valuable concession from them.

Enhancing the cost and value of concessions

A great deal of skill is required on the part of the supplier in raising the apparent *cost to him and value to the buyer* of a concession he is trading. Remember that if there is no apparent cost to you then you are really conceding nothing.

Concessions *from* you *to* the buyer: with these concessions you must credibly *raise* the value to the buyer of the concession you are offering by applying the benefits of the concession to his needs. You can reinforce this value by stressing credibly the high cost of the concession to you. 'You will appreciate that increasing our promotional support to you for this product is not something I could easily agree to considering the cost and how my budget is already heavily committed.'

Concessions *from* the buyer *to* you: similarly the buyer will magnify the costs to him and the value to you of his concessions. You will attempt to qualify these statements by minimising the value to you of his concessions.

Matching and trading concessions

Concessions must be traded carefully. That is to say you must not take your hands off your concession until the buyer has agreed on what he will do in return. (... 'I will do this if you will do that'.) If you habitually refer to your concessions alone, the buyer will accept them without reciprocation.

Maintaining the fabric of the negotiation

In many respects, negotiation is a vital game played for real consequence. Any unduly early attempt by either side to 'dig in their heels' by being genuinely inflexible will be met by reciprocal inflexibility from the other side, and the negotiation will break down. It is critical in these cases that at the conclusion of the negotiation both sides agree they cannot reasonably bridge the gap between them at this stage, or in this instance. Such a conclusion leaves open the possibility of further negotiation on the same subject, or new negotiations in another area. A breakdown in negotiation caused by the unreasonable inflexibility of one party will not leave those possibilities so open for the future. At all times, even when you have reached a point beyond which you are not prepared to go, you must appear to be reasonable. Remember that you are playing a ritual game which is firmly based in hard financial reality. For many buyers much of their sense of achievement comes from playing the game.

The definition of a successful negotiation from the supplier's angle is one which ends on your side of the point of need balance, but where the buyer believes that the deal favours him. The steps and methods to be used in achieving a successful outcome are as follows:

1   Allow the buyer to do most of the talking in the early stages, but don't frustrate him by refusing to answer his questions.

2   Move the discussion from opening stances to a clear statement of actual stances, taking care to limit your losses on both sides. It is your responsibility to 'save face' for the buyer:

(a) A buyer first presents his stance: you have then a variety of possible responses to it:
   (i)   accept it and persuade him that the negatives are greater than the positives;
   (ii) accept it and go back to initial problem with alternatives;
   (iii) ignore it and take own stance;
   (iv) take opposite stance;
   (v)   accept it and use 'suppose' technique.

(b) You present your stance first: you can:
   (i)   take exaggerated view;
   (ii) take actual stance (when your case is strong);
   (iii) 'give' buyer his stance (i.e. indicate your initial acceptance);
   (iv) 'give' both stances in the current environment: both initial; sales initial/buyer actual; both actual.

3   Avoid premature stance on any point which might result in reaching a point of no return too early in the negotiation. It is easier for the buyer to walk away than it is for you in most circumstances.

4   Try to close on a clear statement of the actual gaps between you.

5   Trade any concessions *one at a time*, ensuring that you raise the value of your concessions to him above their cost to you. Make a small move on your part seem large to him.

6   Tactics of devaluing cost to buyer and value to salesman of the buyer's concession, viz.:

(a) treat it as given (assumption) that there is no real concession;
(b) competitors always expect it (or more);
(c) there is benefit to the buyer in agreeing;
(d) 'we've got the benefits anyway';
(e) 'you'd incur the cost anyway';

(f) look for a more major concession then suggest the 'minor' one as an alternative;

(g) it is normal practice.

7   Increasing the value of concessions given to the buyer, and the cost of giving it for the salesman:

(a) imply that you cannot really give it;
(b) refer to major problem that will be solved by the concession;
(c) refer to saving gained by the buyer;
(d) calculate the financial results of the concession;
(e) refer to loss if concession is not given;
(f) refer to past gains from similar concessions;
(g) imply loss that you will incur by giving concessions;
(h) build up notional cost or opportunity cost of giving the concession;
(i) start by implying you are going to give a small concession then give a large one or enlarge the small concession;
(j) not normal practice ('competitors don't do it').

8   Handling situations where the buyer is asking for concession that you cannot give:

(a) build up cost of giving the concession;
(b) minimise the importance to the buyer of the concession;
(c) *persuade* the buyer that the benefits of the deal without the concession still justify acceptance;
(d) offer an alternative concession;
(e) summarise the problem area and offer alternative concession or a choice of alternatives;
(f) show the concession would put the buyer at a disadvantage.

With each and every concession made, whether from you or the buyer, it is essential that *you* summarise the details agreed. This will prevent misinterpretations later. It is further advisable that having agreed the concession details you should make *written* notes.

9   Have facts and figures fluently to hand – but not 'pat' or 'glib' ones.

10   Avoid emotional reactions, but satisfy the buyer's emotional needs. The good buyer/negotiator will try to put you under emotional pressure.

11 Allow the buyer to save face in giving you a concession.

12 Ensure that the buyer is given the 'value satisfaction' he needs, and that you confirm it.

13 At the end of your negotiation interview summarise totally the agreements made, both by you and the buyer.

Conclusion

Negotiation relies on you accurately identifying, at the *preparation* stage:

1 The buyer's needs.
2 Your needs.
3 The point of balance.
4 The value of your concessions to the buyer.
5 The benefits to the buyer of your concessions that will increase their value.
6 The concessions he will give, and how their 'cost' to him can be minimised.
7 The buyer's likely initial stance.
8 How you can move the buyer from his initial stance to the point of balance.

You are then in a position to meet the buyer without fear of conceding points for no reasons. You will be able to meet a point of balance where the buyer is satisfied, and you have achieved your objectives.

The following two examples (Tables 9.1 and 9.2) indicate the chain of negotiations between the supplier and a soft drinks manufacturer and the consequential negotiations between the soft drinks manufacturer and the typical food chain through whom he sells his products.

Table 9.1
The contact between buyer and supplier in the plant
Soft drink situation: supplies

Main negotiating points	Buyer's view	Supplier's view
Quality of supplies being purchased	What variance in quality can be expected from the supplier in question?	How reliable is the production output from our plant?
	Are the variances that may be expected critical to our own process?	Will our plant be able to maintain a consistent supply of material within the accepted quality level?
	Will quality problems at supplier's plant restrict supply and interfere with production of company goods?	What is the quality level of our competitors product?
	Is the quality of the supply favourable to that from competitive suppliers?	What quality aspects can we use to persuade the buyer to take our product in preference to that of our competitors?
	Will the supplier provide goods in accordance with a quality acceptance plan?	Can we agree on a quality acceptance plan with our client?
	Does the supplier employ QC procedures in his plant?	Can our plant adhere to the QAP?
	Are the QC procedures adequate?	What QC procedures are practised in our plant? Are they adequate or will they need to be expanded?

Table 9.1 (continued)

Main negotiating points	Buyer's view	Supplier's view
Price of supplies being purchased	What price negotiations can be made with the supplier in question? Does he hold a monopoly? Does he hold the only patent or agency for the material? Are other sources of supply available? Are volume discounts available? Are package type discounts available?	What price negotiations can we make to the buyer? Are we the only supplier? What other competitors do we have for our range of products? Are we aware of the price/volume discounts of our competitors? What types of packaging are available?
Ability of supplier to maintain adequate supplies	What capacity has the supplier available within his plant? Are any constituents of the product imported? Are there any world shortages of this commodity or any of its constituents? Is there any suspect key point in the suppliers plant that will cause breakdowns, and cut off supplies? What arrangements are made by the supplier if there is a serious breakdown or at annual shutdown of his plant?	What components do we use in the product? Are they easily obtainable? How many suppliers of raw materials are there? Is there an alternative supplier of raw materials? If this material becomes unavailable, is there a similar product we can offer that will perform the same function? What arrangements do we make regarding supplies at times of major breakdown and annual shutdown (if any)?

Main negotiating points	Buyer's view	Supplier's view
Technical specifications for supplies	What specifications are available for the material to be purchased? What processes of manufacture are used? Does the selected supplier use the best process? Are the specification ranges tight enough for our operation? Can the supplier produce product fairly easily within the specification range or will we need to spend labour on monitoring his supply?	What are the product specifications for raw materials used in manufacturing the product for the buyer? Will extreme variance in raw material quality vary specification of final product? Are we able to provide a product specification? Are we able to check that our product conforms with the specification required? Is the process we use the most up to date? If not, what plans are in hand to convert to a more up to date process?
Terms of payment for supplies	What terms are available for payment: 30 day, 60 day or even 90 day credit arrangements? Can we arrange to pay as we use, not for unused stocks? Is there a discount on payments within 30 days, 7 days, etc?	What terms can we offer the buyer that will put us at an advantage? What discounts/rebates can we offer? What is the buyer's credit rating? What are other suppliers' knowledge of his performance? Has he been listed for any adverse

Table 9.1 (continued)

Main negotiating points	Buyer's view	Supplier's view
	Are these annual/quarterly/monthly rebates available on volume? Does supplier have a good credit rating? Is he a reputable organisation?	reason in any credit publication? Is the buyer a profitable, liquid company and what are its immediate performance projections?
Stockholding of supplies	What stocks of material are held by the supplier in terms of week's cover of our production? Do we have to hold any stock? What maximum and minimum levels does the supplier work to? What stocks of important ingredients does the supplier hold? Will outside warehouse space be required?	What warehouse space is available that can be allocated to the buyer's product? What does this mean in terms of the buyer's plant production days? What stocks of raw materials can we hold? What is the recovery time of our plant in regard to replenishment of stock levels? Will outside warehouse space be required? How will the above affect the price of the product and has it been allowed?
Packaging of supplies	What range of packaging is available? Is there a range of cheaper bulk packages? Is there a bulk delivery facility?	What range of packaging material can we use for this product? Is it the most convenient? Are there other mediums available?

Main negotiating points	Buyer's view	Supplier's view
	What degree of handling does the packaging of the material withstand? Can material be handled easily within plant? Can it be removed easily from packaging without losses?	Will it stand up to handling? Can it be conveniently handled by the buyer? Can the buyer take bulk deliveries. Can we supply the product in bulk? What future plans are in hand to improve supply?
Delivery of supplies	How is material delivered (packs, pallets etc.)? Is there returnable packaging involved? Who does the delivery? Is freight an additional cost to quoted price? Can national FIS price be arranged? Is delivery service reliable? Can urgent deliveries be made? How is return of suspect product arranged?	Is our delivery fleet working to full capacity, or can problems be seen in not meeting prompt delivery times? Is any special type of truck required to deliver the goods (e.g. what can supplier handle)? Can contractors be used? What is our current reputation in the trade for meeting delivery targets? Do we have to rely on other instrumentalities to provide transport (rail, shipping)? Has adequate provision been made in our costing for product delivery?

Table 9.2

The contact between buyer and seller in foodchain
Typical soft drink situation

Main negotiating points	Buyer's view	Seller's view
Price of supply, terms and conditions	Seeking stability of price and additional discounts and deals. To ensure we get the best price in relation to our competitors. We are aiming for maximum turnover with high profit per unit sale. Best possible credit facilities and terms. We are advised as early as possible on price increases or other charges relating to price and terms.	To obtain maximum price from dealer consistent with fullest support and stocking capacity. To keep tabs on competitive terms and conditions. To ensure they are not gaining an advantage with buyer. To ensure documentation flows smoothly.
Delivery	Reliability of delivery. Goods properly identified on delivery notes. Delivery at times convenient to buyer. No hold up to supplies. We want prompt service.	Ensure we have sufficient floor stocks. That potential stock problems are known in advance so buyer may be notified. We have dependable delivery service with minimum union problems and other disruptions.

Main negotiating points	Buyer's view	Seller's view
Stockholding levels	Minimum stocking levels required commensurate with sales off-take. To guard against overstock but take advantage vendor's deals when available.	To ensure maximum stocking levels in order to force and maintain high distribution and stocks at forward selling areas.
Defective and obsolete stocks	Ensure replacements carried out effectively. To ensure slow sellers are liquidated with supplier's participation. We want prompt service in this area and if product doesn't sell to be able to return to vendor.	Whilst offering a replacement service keep returns to a minimum and ensure that job lines are kept to absolute minimum by alerting buyers to situation in his stores. We don't want to take back stock unless absolutely necessary.
Store merchandising and distribution	To permit supplier's merchandisers into our stores to help with stock replacement and merchandising. This saves us labour providing it is properly controlled. Supplies must not overstep our	Excellent opportunity to do PR job with section leader and store manager. We aim to have maximum shelf exposure and displays. Also to cement relations down the line. Educate section leader to advantages

Table 9.2 (continued)

Main negotiating points	Buyer's view	Seller's view
	of stocking our product – to obtain maximum shelf and off-location display space. Also merchandiser's presence must not disrupt our operation in any way.	company policy in respect of allotted shelf facings and display material, etc. Also good opportunity for intelligence work on competition (i.e. checking competitive price 'specialling' – new products, etc.).
Co-operative advertising	We wish to obtain maximum support from the supplier in monetary terms so our prices may be discounted and co-operative advertising and promotion may be arranged. To ensure the participants in our total co-operative advertising package are major lead lines where 'specialling' will bring the customers into our stores.	To maximise our share of total availability of soft drink promotional programme. To ensure our company focuses attention on to the right products/brands (the largest and most profitable). To ensure that our co-operative advertising programmes are policed – they are carried out in accordance with our pre-agreed plan. Also to provide fullest on-the-spot help in the form of store merchandising.
Contact	Phone orders to plant are handled efficiently. Are personal calls	We need to keep best possible rapport with buyer and HO personnel so that

Main negotiating points	Buyer's view	Supplier's view
	necessary – we are busy. There must be a purpose to the call. We are interested in industry trends by flavour and package and what our competitors are doing.	our product is uppermost in their minds and we gain maximum support. We also need to form close liaison at store level to get best results possible. This contact is a useful source of competitive information.
Packaging and warehousing	Packaging must be convenient size and shape and easily disposed of. Ease of warehouse handling, fork on, fork off. We need to minimise breakages and spillages and packages must be easily identifiable for warehouse picking, and packaging must be robust and withstand humidity and heat.	We must make sure our packaging reaches forward selling areas. Identification of contents must be good otherwise they are overlooked by warehousemen. Packages must be robust so that stock reaches store racks in mint condition. Poor presentation puts customers off.
Variety of product to be carried	To confine selling range to minimum variety and size consistent with maximum turnover. At same time to	To maximise range so far as possible, to achieve maximum shelf facings to detriment of competitive brands.

Table 9.2 (continued)

Main negotiating points	Buyer's view	Supplier's view
	take into consideration our involvement with major competitors in similar product category.	
The new product/packaging introduction	Caution in purchase of new lines, reassurance needed regarding off-take. Why should we stock product? If really new product, has it been test marketed? In the case of 'me too's' why should we stock this product in preference to established products because we are sure to delete something else to put a 'me too' in? The 'me too' has to be cheaper than established product or have a real and definite advantage. We want to know how the product will be advertised, where and when and how long the ads will last. We also require samples. We require information about how many	Most important to obtain maximum co-operation right at start. We need largest possible opening order to force maximum shelf facings and distribution through all stores. We need co-operative advertising promotion to achieve maximum publicity coincidentally with start of advertising campaign. Our objective must be to get buyer to ensure that all outlets are thoroughly briefed on details of new product and importance of launch. To obtain best store grading (classification) with the new product we are offering.

Main negotiating points	Buyer's view	Supplier's view
	products to a carton and how big the outer carton is – how many cartons to a layer – and layers to a pallet. We do not wish to see elaborate presentations in our office – or sit and watch TV ads. We don't have the time. What are the prices for quantity buys including any opening deals and how long will the deals last?	

In chapter 5 the differences between negotiation and selling are defined and examined in detail; and on pages 71-93 an interview between a salesman selling and a buyer buying, the latter using negotiating techniques skilfully, is reproduced verbatim. Now we give another verbatim interview with the same commercial situation *but this time the salesman has been trained to negotiate.*

Example of a salesman trained in negotiation techniques negotiating with a trained buyer

The commercial situation

This is identical to the one described on pp. 71-93. But there are two vital differences in the salesman, Mr Edmunds. Firstly, he has now been trained to negotiate deals of the type he is handling here; secondly (and arising from this), his negotiating objectives for this *key* meeting are now related to the profitability of the order rather than whether he gets an order at any price.

Buyer's objectives	*Salesman's objectives*
To obtain the best possible machines for his company on time to meet his company's financial and marketing plans. This company's machines are of the best quality and he will try and negotiate their purchase on the following terms:	To sell the ten new machines at the quotation price.
1 To obtain the machines with the guarantee that 'C' part spares stock unused are taken back by the manufacturer at the end of twelve months free of charge.	1 To arrange for the machines to be delivered to Birmingham within the price allowed for in the quotation. 2 To supply the recommended parts stock to the level specified in the quotation.
2 To have the machines painted before delivery in the company's new	3 To obtain some form of public relations value from the supply of the new machines by trading help with the training of operators or painting them in the company's livery.

The discussion	Notes

livery free of charge.
3 To have the machines delivered to a number of different depots rather than all to one depot and so avoid carrying the cost of onward delivery.
4 To have the operators and fitters responsible for the new machines trained on a special course laid on by the manufacturer free of charge.
5 To obtain the manufacturer's agreement in writing to a guaranteed buy-back figure.
6 To obtain a discount of 2½ per cent off the quoted price of each machine.

4 To ensure that arrangements are made to train the new machinery operators to correspond with the dates of delivery.

The costs involved in the transaction

1 Quoted price of machines: £11,500 each: 10 × £11,500 = £115,000.
2 Initial cost of recommended parts stock: £4,100 ('C' part spare value £2,800).
3 Cost of paint-spraying each new machine: £35 per machine.
4 Cost of delivering ten machines to one point (Birmingham): £700.
5 Cost of delivery to separate points: minimum £100 per machine to a distance of 100 miles from plant (any distance over that 50p per mile extra).
6 Cost of operator training at company's training school: £35 per delegate.

The discussion	Notes

Buyer   Good morning Mr Edmunds, please sit down.

Salesman	Good morning Mr Johnson. Thank you. You have our quote and so I hope we can reach a decision today because the demand on these new machines could put back your chances of delivery quite seriously otherwise.	Salesman tries to close on original quotation.
B	Well I hope we can reach a decision too today, but in order to get to that stage there are some items in your quotation I would like to deal with.	Buyer indicates desire to reach an agreement provided terms are acceptable.
S	Fine. What are they?	Salesman asks for details.
B	Well let me deal first of all with the areas where I think we are all right. As far as the technical specification is concerned, and the machine capability, I am quite satisfied and so are our technical people. There are no problems there whatsoever. The areas where I think we need to have some discussions are in the total package as opposed simply to the machine itself.	
	I am talking about bringing the machines in and then developing the staff and these types of things. Those are the areas where we need to talk because at the moment although I	Buyer tries not to be too explicit, except to emphasise the uncompetitiveness of the quotation and thus disconcert the sales-man.

am quite happy with the
technical side of the
operation, competitively
you are a bit weak on the
other aspects.

S   Well let's have a look
at them, shall we?
Can we take them all
and then we can look
at them in the round?

Salesman asks for *all*
the points, so that
he has a full idea of
what is involved.

B   Well I think there are
some that are of major
importance and others
that I would call of
peripheral importance.
Perhaps we could deal
with the major things first
of all. One of them is the
recommended parts stock.

Buyer identifies one
point only:
Parts stock.

S   Yes, what concerns you
there?

Salesman asks for details.

B   Well, as you know, these
are new machines but they
are also new models, and I
think quite understandably
in that situation your
recommended parts stock
is much higher both in
value and in volume than
one would normally have
for a standard machine.
That places on us a
considerable financial
commitment which I am
not prepared to accept *in
toto* at this point in time
and I think we need to
talk about how we can get
that financial commitment
down in some way or
other.

The discussion	Notes

S Fine, that's point 1, and what's next?

B I mean what would you suggest as far as parts volume is concerned?

S Well, what I am suggesting just at this stage is let's take all the points because after all, as you say, we are looking at a total package. Let's take all of them. I think some of them will relate one to another.

B Right.

S Therefore shall we talk about all of them in one go?

B Well I certainly think as far as you're concerned this parts stock area and the value of it is something we need to look at in some detail.

S Oh I'm sure we do.

B A second area is this question of delivery. Now when I spoke to you last time, I think you were under the impression that we would have delivery to our Birmingham depot. Since then we have had discussions with the regional managers in the other centres and it is clear that they have a demand in those centres,

Notes:

Salesman asks for other points before dealing with the parts stock.

Buyer tries to get the parts stock cleared up before revealing the rest of his hand.

Salesman refuses to be sidetracked. He needs the total picture so that he can identify the size of the gap between them and thus the mid-point where agreement should be reached.

Buyer reveals second point: *Delivery.*

and also we feel that it is
important that they should
have the opportunity to
try them out so that we
can determine just what is
the demand in those areas,
so that if and when we
decide to purchase more
machines we will know
where to place them and
how many we need.

S   Well how would you   Salesman asks for details.
dispose of the ten?

B   Well of the ten I have the
split here. Three would go
to Birmingham, as we
originally agreed.

S   Yes...

B   We shall need three in   Buyer minimises the
London, two in   problems created by
Manchester, one in   his request.
Glasgow and one in
Plymouth. Now I imagine
from your point of view
that delivery to these
centres doesn't present any
major problems.

S   It doesn't present a   Salesman indicates
major problem, it does   willingness to talk,
present a certain amount   without committing
of cost and availability   himself.
of transport but that's
fine, let's come to that
as well.

B   You think you can meet   Buyer seeks agreement.
that one?

S   I'm quite sure we can   Salesman agrees that the
deliver to those areas   delivery arrangements
or that we can make sure   can be changed but
that the machines arrive   does not commit his
in those areas. That   company to paying for it.

won't be a problem.

B   Good. The other major
area is the question of
the way in which we
dispose of these machines
when they come to the
end of their normal life.
As you know, our policy
is that after two years we
normally sell them off.
Now in this particular
case, bearing in mind that
they are new models, what
I would like to do is to
adopt the policy of many
of your customers which is
to have some form of buy-
back arrangement with
you.

Buyer raises third point:
Buy-back.

S   Yes.

B   And so we need to come
to some agreement on the
level at which you would
be prepared to take these
back from us after two
years.

S   Now those are the main
points are they?

Salesman checks that
there are no other
major points for
discussion.

B   Yes.

S   Now what about the minor
ones. Were there any
significant ones?

He now moves to the
minor ones.

B   No I don't think so.
One concerns livery –
we will need to have them
painted in our new colours
which is a result of the
corporate image study we
have done.

Buyer raises fourth point:
Livery.

The discussion

S   Is the basic colour still yellow?

B   No it isn't. There will be a certain degree of yellow in it but the predominant colour will be green, Lincoln green.

S   Which would mean us clearing out a paint shop and doing a total new job.

B   That's right. But I would imagine that you've done that in the past.

S   We have done it indeed. Yes, yes.

B   We shall need to have that done – free of charge of course. And the other peripheral area is the question of operator training. I know that it is normal policy to train operators to operate the machines. In our particular case we're talking about two or three people per regional centre which means twelve to fifteen people in all. But in addition we want to be sure that the people who are going to maintain these machines are trained at the same time so that both operators and fitters are familiar with them. So we're talking altogether about something like twenty/twenty-five people that need to be trained.

Notes

Salesman stresses the cost of the change.

Buyer plays it down.

Buyer raises fifth point: *Training*.

The discussion

S I see.

B I think I may be able to
save you a headache here.
Normally you would pull
people in one at a time?

S That's right, yes.

B And in pulling people
in one at a time you have
this problem that you
are mixing them with
other people's staff.
I wouldn't want this
to happen because I
don't want our com-
petitors to know
quickly that we are
anticipating this purchase.
And I certainly don't want
them to know what we've
got in the way of
maintenance facilities and
maintenance procedures.
So what I would like to
do is to have a
programme purely for our
own people and I think
the best way to do this is
for us to lay it on at our
own depot in Birmingham,
which is close to you.
We'll provide all the
facilities, accommodation
and everything else and all
you need to do is to lay
on a trainer, to provide
the necessary training aids
and also a machine for
demonstration and
training purposes.

S So we have these five
points:
    1 the parts stock;

Notes

Buyer explains why he
  wants special treatment.

Buyer implies that, as
  he is making the
  arrangements for the
  training, the supplier's
  role is considerably
  reduced.

Salesman checks the complete
  picture. He now knows the nature

The discussion

2 the delivery;
3 the buy-back;
4 the paint job;
5 the operator training.

B That's right. And of those
the parts stock, delivery
and buy-back I think are
the most important.

S Good. Well let's examine
those because certainly
there is quite a lot we
can do for you in these
areas. Can we take this
parts stock one first
because it is in many ways
separate from the others?
When we talk about parts
stock we are talking
presumably about the slow
moving, the 'C' class
spares?

B That's right. As you well
know the 'A' and 'B' class
spares are common to
other machines. I'm
mainly concerned about
the 'C' class spares which
are peculiar to this
machine, and I don't want
to have a situation where
at the end of twelve
months we have got a lot
of 'C' parts on hand which
we won't need to use, and
therefore I would like to
agree that at the end of

Notes

and financial impli-
cations of the buyer's
requests and can
decide how to handle
them, how big is the
gap between them, and
where the mid point
lies where agreement
should be reached.

Salesman *chooses* to
deal with parts stock
first.

He asks for clarification.

Buyer explains.

twelve months any that we
haven't used of the 'C'
part you will take back
free of charge.

S   Well, I think there's
no reason we cannot
help you here. The quote
includes 'A' and 'B' spares
doesn't it?

Salesman is willing to
be reasonable.

B   Yes quite clearly there will
be 'A' and 'B' type spares
that we already have.

S   Yes, there will. You
know the thing that
troubles me slightly.
Obviously things like
basic split pins I'm
not so concerned about.
Indeed I think that in our
original parts stock for
these machines we haven't
excluded these spare parts
altogether. But if you are
willing to take from us the
total parts stock
recommended both on the
'A' and 'B' and the 'C'
class spares, I see no
reason why we should not
guarantee a buy-back on
the 'C' class spares at the
end of twelve months;
unless, of course, you
want to maintain that
stock at that stage for
further machines that you
are likely to buy.

Salesman offers a
concession, provided
that the buyer will
take the total recom-
mended stock.

B   Yes, I think that's
fair. If you can guarantee
that you will take back
any unused 'C' parts at the

Buyer agrees.

end of twelve months free
of charge then we will be
prepared to take the
recommended total spares
that you have laid out in
your quotation.

S That's fine. Now I am
sure that's a wise
decision because the
machine is new, and needs
even in the smaller areas
the precise part that is
necessary. That will help
your people considerably
with the fitting manuals
because the parts numbers
will correspond.

S The delivery points do
trouble me somewhat. You
have run low loaders
perhaps even more than
we do and you know the
kinds of costs. The
original costs that we
put in were based on
delivery to Birmingham.
This is what we were
building in. I don't
think that it is necessarily
too great a problem and
we could handle it one of
two ways. First, we could
agree that you collected,
and you could collect very
simply with your
Plymouth loader taking
two and dropping one in
London, and your
Glasgow loader taking two
and dropping one in
Birmingham. If you were

Salesman reinforces the
buyer's decision.

Salesman takes the
initiative, and intro-
duces the point of:
Delivery.

He offers two alter-
natives to meet the
buyer's requirements
but asks for reciprocal
movement from the
buyer.

to collect, then we could
remove altogether the,
well it's about 0.7 per cent
but let's say 1 per cent,
from our quote.
Alternatively, we discuss
an economic rate for
adjusting the delivery costs
as you now require them.

B   Well, I think I need
at this stage to put
you in the picture as
far as the competitors
are concerned. As you
well know, there are
several machines on the
market which we could
take as very suitable for
this application. I think
the significant difference is
that they are prepared to
deliver these quantities to
the regional centres free of
charge.

Buyer decides to use
the competitive
'stick' to beat a
better deal out of
the salesman.

S   That doesn't surprise me
at all. Indeed with the
demand that we have got
for the 787 I can quite
see that they are prob-
ably getting a bit
desperate anyway. My
problem is not just with
the cost, though that's
part of it. My problem
is one of capacity. You
know very well what it
costs to keep a low
loader on the road, and
we quoted on the basis
that the total delivery
would be to Birmingham,

Salesman stresses the
difficulties in
delivering to several
points. He suggests an
alternative method:
a reduced price in
exchange for delivery
when it suits his own
company.

which from
Wolverhampton is a very
easy and simple trip to
manage. I doubt that I
could really pull together
the low loader capacity to
cope with so many
locations at once. What
we could do is take the
situation as it runs and on
these longer trips prolong
delivery somewhat to the
end of January, or early
February, and in that way
still deliver at a much
reduced delivery charge.

B   How much? You said 0.7
per cent.

S   Yes 0.7 per cent to
1 per cent. I think I
could arrange for us to
simply deliver within
what we have already built
into the quote and make
no extra charge if you
were willing to delay
delivery by about six
weeks. On the other hand,   He offers a further
if you've now got low   alternative: No charge
loaders running light, as I   for delivery if the
imagine that in several of   customer collects.
your depots you will have
at this time of the year, I
would be quite happy for
them to come and collect
and take that out of our
quotation. The choice is
really with you, but I
would recommend that
you took the earlier

delivery. The sooner you
get these machines on the
ground, the sooner you
get the element of surprise
which is available to you
with a new machine.

B   I think on balance,   Customer accepts the
     Mr Edmunds, I would   first alternative.
     prefer your previous
     suggestion. If you can
     deliver to these centres at
     this reduced rate then I
     am prepared to accept
     delivery for some of them
     towards the end of
     January.

S   Yes, I can do that.

B   Good.

S   Now, I will have to go
     back and re-check our
     production scheduling
     because they won't be
     exactly the same machines
     which I had scheduled for
     building mid-December.

B   They meet the
     specifications?

S   Oh yes they will still be   Salesman now decides to
     787s. Now, the next point   tackle:
     you had was buy-back. It   *Buy-back*.
     is not our normal practice
     with a plant-hire company   He argues for an inde-
     to produce a buy-back   pendent valuation in
     price. The reasons I   two years' time rather
     think are obvious. Some   than fixing a figure
     of the old machines   now.
     naturally get a great deal
     more wear than others,
     and this is why you not
     only maintain such an up-
     to-date fleet, but also

change your machines
frequently. However, as
arrangements stand, we
would be willing at the
end of two years to re-
purchase these machines
on an independent
appraisal of their full
market value. To produce
a figure now might be
unfair to you or rather
dangerous for my
company, which naturally
I would be unwilling to
do. More worrying is that
in two years' time you
might be able to make
much better arrangements
elsewhere, because of the
low usage or the very well-
handled usage. We would
therefore be prepared to
buy back on an
independent valuation at
that time.

B   I appreciate what you're   Buyer asks for a price
saying, but I think we   now.
need to understand that
plant-hire contractors do
have buy-back
arrangements with
manufacturers. In our
particular case, although
we have had this
arrangement with other
people, we have never
invoked it. In terms of an
arrangement it is nothing
new. I was hoping that
what you would be able to
do would be to give us a

guaranteed buy-back price
now based on a
percentage of the purchase
price that you've quoted.

S   That, of course, we could
do, and that I would be
quite willing to do. I
think, however, that the
price which we would be
liable to present to you
would not be altogether
acceptable. That is why I
suggested the independent
assessment in two years'
time. Because of all the
improbables involved,
such as type of conditions,
type of operator, the
economic situation, new
machine introduction,
government grant, etc., I
don't think we could do
you a fair job at this
moment in time. I agree
with you there are
companies who do
produce buy-back figures,
but whether they are fair
or whether they are trade
allowances in another
form is, as you know very
well, another matter
altogether.

Salesman stresses the
disadvantages to the
buyer of fixing a
price now.

B   What sort of figure are
you thinking of?
S   Figure of what?
B   A buy-back figure. You
say an independent
valuation. Would you be
prepared to accept that it
would be either a certain

Buyer tries to get the
best of both worlds.

figure or the valuation,
whichever was the greater?

S   Well, that doesn't really
solve the problem. That
safeguards your side but
it doesn't safeguard
my side. I think the
independent valuation
would be at market rate at
the time. You have taken
a forward view of the
market as we have. At
present there is a demand
in the market, but whether
in two years' time that's
going to still be the same,
or whether we'll be in
recession, or whether we'll
be in a buoyant situation
is very difficult to say.
What I'm trying to do is
to produce the fairest
situation for both of us.
Our used machinery
division are selling at best
prices and would be quite
happy to buy on an
independent market rate,
and whether we really
broke even on it or in fact
lost money that's up to
them. That really doesn't
bother me. What does
bother me is agreeing a
price now.

B   But you will be prepared
to accept a completely
independent valuation?

S   Yes, indeed.

B   And if we could get a
better deal ourselves

Salesman senses that the
buyer's position is
not very strong and
therefore presses his
point home.

selling it off elsewhere that
would be all right?

S   We would be very happy
for you.

B   Then on that basis I   Buyer accepts salesman's
think we can agree.   proposal.

S   Good. Now there are two
other points I think
that you mentioned at
the beginning. We called
them peripheral points
but I think they are in
fact quite important and
quite difficult too. The
first was this paint job. Of   Salesman turns to:
course we can do a livery   *Livery*.
job and indeed we do
often do it, though   First, he makes it clear
naturally we normally   that a change is not
charge for it. After all it   as simple as it sounds.
means stopping the paint
shop, cleaning the guns,
and getting the whole
thing set up.

One thing does occur to   Then he suggests a *quid*
me. I was talking to my   *pro quo*: the pos-
Advertising Manager the   sibility of free paint-
other day about this job   ing in the new colours
and he was saying how   in exchange for joint
interesting it would be,   PR.
and I think for your PR
people as well, if in trying
to promote your corporate
image and in trying to
gain the public relations
value that we want for this
new machine, we were
able to come to some
arrangement whereby we
could use the machines, in
your livery, in the local

and national press,
certainly in something like
Contracts Journal, and
generate PR value from it.
If you could work that out
with your advertising
people I reckon I might be
able to persuade our
people to accept the paint
job free of charge.

B　I think from your point
of view that may seem
relatively simple,
Mr Edmunds. In fact it
is asking quite a lot
because, as a plant-hire
organisation, we have to
be extremely careful in
our relationship with the
manufacturers that we are
not seen to tie ourselves
too closely to any one of
them. I don't want us to
get into a situation where
we are badgered right, left
and centre to take
machines in exchange for
free advertising. However,
this point about corporate
image could be – I'm not
saying that it will be – but
it could be of interest.
What I would need to do
is to talk to our own
advertising manager to see
how far he would be
prepared to go along with
it. But I certainly think it's
an area that we could talk
about.

S　Good. Clearly, we would

Buyer stresses the
problem it would create
for his company, but
recognises the possible
value of such an
arrangement.

have to liaise on things
like copy and both of us
would want to make sure
that we were getting from
it what we wanted. I
doubt whether that is such
a major problem. If you
can arrange it, I will
undertake to get the paint
job through for you.

B   Well, let's put it this   Buyer seeks a long-term
way. If we were to agree,   concession in return
it would be a major   for joint PR.
departure from policy.
Consequently, I would
need a commitment from
you that subsequent
machines would be
painted in our livery free
of charge.

S   That, I think, would have   Salesman accepts.
to follow. Now, the training
is a very difficult one.   Salesman now turns to:
I quite understand your   *Training*.
desire to get it. Indeed,
this is why I was wanting
you to take the machines
earlier. Let's see how this
strikes you. You want   He offers to run a
your men on a special   tailored course, but
course for this machine,   over a weekend. This
with no outsiders. You   will avoid having to
want it done certainly   make a lot of special
in early December, and   arrangements and
you want it done with the   moving the equipment
necessary machines, all   etc. out of the training
the equipment and   centre.
everything else there, and
with properly qualified
trainers.

Now, if you can get
your people together, over
a weekend, either
Friday/Saturday or
Saturday/Sunday (it's a
two-day course), in
Wolverhampton instead of
Birmingham, then I will
make sure that you have
the whole of the centre to
yourselves. We will
provide the machines, lay
on everything else that
you need, give them a
good time, and generally
look after them. That way,
I think that we could
probably manage the
training without too much
trouble. That way, we
wouldn't have to release
that machine out, and
getting hold of a machine
of course is almost
impossible. But do you
think you could get them
to come?

B   Oh there's no problem in   Buyer asks for a
getting them in. The   reduced cost per head
problem is that if we get   to compensate for
men in over the weekend,   overtime payments.
they are going to want the
rate for the job: time and
a half Saturdays, double
time Sundays. Now, in
order to pay them that
kind of money, I imagine
you'd be quite prepared,
particularly in view of the
fact that you're using your
centre over the weekends

which normally you don't
do, so you're getting
added mileage out of it, to
come to some
arrangement on the cost
of carrying out this
training? In other words,
some form of reduction in
the course fee per head
would go some way to
subsidising the cost of
taking these men out of
their normally free
weekends?

S　Well, if we took Friday/
Saturday that would
mean your cost would
not be quite so high,
and your staffing is
not quite so heavy at the
beginning of December. If
you could do that, then I
think we could discount
the costs of the training by
20 per cent. We would
carry our own staff costs
and we wouldn't make any
extra charge for having
the staff over the weekend.
Yes, I think we could do
that for you.

　　　　　　Salesman offers a
　　　　　　reduced fee if the
　　　　　　buyer can agree to
　　　　　　a course on a Friday
　　　　　　and Saturday.

B　Well on that basis I
would be very happy.

　　　　　　Buyer agrees.

S　So, if we take the parts
stock: we will supply
the 'C' class spares
and take them back at the
end of twelve months if
you buy to the full
recommended parts stock
level on the 'A' and 'B'

　　　　　　Salesman now summarises
　　　　　　all the points that
　　　　　　have been covered.

spares. On delivery, we will work on that slightly extended period so that we can fit it in with our availability of loading and we'll make sure the last machine is with you by end of first week in February.

B   And all machines will be delivered free?

S   All machines delivered as they are already standing in the plant. No extra charge. On buy-back, we will take an independent valuation at the end of two years, if you still want it then.

B   We will both take an independent valuation!

S   Fine, in fact if you have an independent valuer, we will take his valuation. On paint: if you can get your advertising people to agree the PR usage, we will manage the paint job free. On training: if the two of us can agree a Saturday early in December, then we will provide the training with 20 per cent off our nominal charge. On that basis perhaps we ought to think about going ahead. As I said to you at the beginning, I'm very worried that with the production schedule going forward there could be

problems if we don't sign
up today. So do you think
we can go ahead?

B   I think so. There's one
thing I would like to
discuss with you before
we make any full commit-
ment and that is this.
These are brand-new
machines, brand-new
models; this is the first
time we shall have had
them, the first time in fact
anybody in the market has
had them. You've also
suggested this idea of joint
advertising. I'm not a
marketing man and you
know this far better than I
do, but I would imagine
that if you're going to do
that kind of mixed or
joint advertising the last
thing you can afford,
having blown your
trumpet, is to find that
you've missed a few notes.
That being the case I
think it's important to
both of us that, in
addition to the things
we've already agreed, we
as a company should be
upgraded to the level
whereby if anything
should go wrong in the
field that our people can't
cope with, you will give us
the level of service that
your grade 1 customers
get. By that I mean that

Salesman closes.
Seeing the salesman's
    desire to get the
    order, buyer throws
    in an unexpected
    demand:
    Service upgrading.

your people will come out
at a moment's notice, day
or night, seven days a
week and put things right
for us. Now if you can do
that, I might well be in the
position to get this pushed
through quickly.
Obviously this level of
capital expenditure needs
board approval, but if we
could just add that to the
package that we have
agreed today, I think I
could get it through by the
weekend.

Mind you my managing   Buyer suggests that the
director will take a   order is there if only
pretty tough view of   the salesman will
the agreement we've   accept this final
reached because he   request.
will probably feel that we
might have been able to
do better elsewhere.

S   So what you are asking us
    for is a special technical
    back-up support
    programme?

B   No, not a special one.   Buyer emphasises that
    Just the normal level   other customers get it.
    of service enjoyed by
    your grade 1 customers.

S   Well, I will stick my   Salesman builds up the
    neck out and agree to   value and difficulty
    this order being clas-   of the unexpected
    sified as qualifying   demand, though actual
    for grade 1 customer   cost is small.
    technical support service   Reluctantly agrees.
    provided you can confirm
    in writing over the
    weekend, together with the

    arrangement about the
parts spares, the joint
publicity on the painting,
and the training course.
You will appreciate that in
making this offer I am
taking a considerable
decision on behalf of our
technical service director.

B   Fine, Mr Edmunds. Subject   The deal is concluded.
to the board approval,
which I do not feel will
present any problems, I
will send you confirmation
of this order and the
points we have agreed by
Monday.

Table 9.3
Negotiation tactics: check-list

Tactic	Comment
1 If you know your objectives don't be afraid to start suggesting major terms.	You know what your next move is.
2 Always start high and trade down.	Use your highest figures first then trade down if you have to. You can rarely trade up from a lower figure.
3 Conceal your emotions.	Try and keep a poker face. Avoid expressing relief, disgust, elation. It will give clues to your opponent. If you do any of these things it becomes an act which it is difficult to sustain for long.

Tactic	Comment
4 Use silence.	When an unacceptable offer is presented, silence is the best reply.
5 Be prepared to break off negotiation when the alternative is having to retract later.	If the unexpected arises, it is better to confer with your colleagues, if there are others in your team, and agree the next step than to go on and then have to retract in front of your opponents.
6 Delay sensitive issues to avoid confrontation.	If you risk a direct confrontation by raising a delicate issue early either delay, or if necessary defer meeting.
7 If a negotiation is deferred decide basis for next meeting.	Always agree the next step or objective if more than one meeting is necessary to reach agreement.
8 Don't exaggerate facts.	Never exaggerate what can later be verified about your company. *Be frank*.
9 When agreement is reached leave.	To delay your departure can expose you to danger of someone wanting to revise the terms of an agreement.
10 Respect buyer's conventions.	Be watchful to ensure you do not offend: 'When in Rome do as the Romans do'.
11 Use simple language.	Negotiation above all else requires clear thinking and clear speech. Keep your language simple.

Table 9.3 (continued)

Tactic	Comment
12 Don't be greedy.	Everyone has his breaking point. If you push too far or too hard you may succeed *once* but only once.

Table 9.4
Negotiation details: Check-list

Detail	Comment
1 Record all points agreed as you go.	Avoid the need to meet again to renegotiate what was not noted down.
2 Keep negotiating team even.	Don't be overpowered or overpower.
3 Choose negotiating team carefully.	How technical will the discussions become? Take technicians for technical advice *only*.
4 Don't assume anything.	Clarify each point agreed including the limits and the precise latitudes.
5 Don't send subordinates to speak for you if you can help it. If you must delegate, make sure you confirm your subordinates' authority in writing, stating the scope and limits of their power.	As a rule, only equals should negotiate. Besides, what your subordinates say they said, and what they *actually* said, rarely are the same.

Detail	Comment
6 Negotiate on your own ground.	But if your objective is to get to know your opposite number visit him on his home ground.
7 Don't embarrass others who make mistakes.	Don't draw attention to their errors and don't knock other people. If you make mistakes don't over-react but don't make too many.
8 Avoid personal opinion about others.	Unless you know people very well your personal opinions can swing a fine-balanced decision against you. Be sure that you understand the 'chemistry of vibrations'.
9 Expect negative reactions in negotiating.	No one wants to give the impression of pleasure at decisions reached in case it alters balance of advantage.

Table 9.5
Negotiation warnings: check-list

Warning	Comment
1 If you decide to be provocative or unpleasant know what you are doing.	Such actions should be very controlled. If you make someone lose their temper they could cause you to lose yours and you may throw away all your negotiating advantages.

Table 9.5 (continued)

Warning	Comment
2 Watch for wandering eyes.	Some people are very good at reading upside down print. They may read your next negotiating point and answer it before you are ready.
3 Don't sign anything in haste.	Always read the small print. It can often contain unnegotiated surprises.
4 Avoid the hospitality trap.	Try and negotiate before lunch.
5 Never be superior.	In negotiating stick to *your objectives*. If you can't reach the minimum, the timing is wrong or your overtures are unwelcome. Better to lose with a good grace and live to parley on a better day.

10 Making effective presentations

Historically, salesmen have been trained to deal with sales situations involving, in the majority of cases, selling to one buyer. In these one-to-one sales/negotiating meetings, there is usually a degree of informality and above all feedback from the buyer in the form of questions and answers to questions. Now the salesman must be equipped to deal skilfully and successfully with group selling and negotiating meetings on an increasing scale. If you are not equipped and prepared for such challenges then you will consciously or unconsciously avoid group meetings even when opportunities arise. There are two main hurdles or fears you will have to overcome in preparing yourself to handle such multiple-sales challenges. First, the risk of being exposed to cross-questioning if you actively seek feedback from qualified technical people; and second, the lack of any evidence of success when making set presentations or speeches.

These two areas must be controlled or eliminated if you want to seize the opportunities these group-selling meetings offer you to sell effectively and successfully to a large number of people at one time. To help you to do this let us consider the main questions involved.

Who becomes involved in buying and selling decisions?

In both buying and selling situations, many people are involved in decisions:

Buying companies	Selling companies
Directors	Sales directors
Purchasing officers/buyers	Salesmen
Marketing staff	Sales managers
Technical staff	Marketing/product managers
Production staff	Technical advisers
Quality control staff	Installers/contractors
Operations/distribution staff	Distribution specialists
Computer staff	Financial analysts
Accountants	Computer staff
	Operations/distribution staff

Who should make or take part in group meetings/presentations?

Great care must be taken to choose the 'best' team to attend such group meetings or to make group presentations so that the subsequent buyer relationships run smoothly. The following factors should be borne in mind:

1   What type of meeting is it?
2   What will be the status and decision-making powers of those present from the buying group?
3   What type of decisions will the meeting reach?
4   What technical expertise will the meeting possess in the buying group? What therefore will it require from your side?
5   Can one man handle the meeting or should a group attend?
6   If a buying decision is likely to be made at meeting, who will run or service the resulting contract?
7   If a group is to present to the buying group, who should lead the group?

Remember: (a) that the on-going relationships with the customer will require the build-up and establishment of credibility of whoever will be chosen for this role; (b) the internal motivation of the salesman/sales team must be considered.

What planning is necessary?

The planning of such group meetings and presentations should cover two stages: first, the planning and preparation stage; second, the conduct and execution stage.

Planning and preparation. There are two sets of factors to be reviewed at the planning and preparation stage: the objective/business elements and the subjective or human elements. The latter are the more difficult but if overlooked can not only ruin one meeting but reduce the chances of a second one ever taking place.

1   *Objective factors*

(a) What results do you want the meeting to achieve?
(b) What will you present and discuss to reach this objective?
(c) How will you present them?
(d) In what order will you present them?
(e) What key questions will you ask?
(f) In what order/at what stage should they be asked?
(g) What visual/display material should be prepared?
(h) How will it be used?

2   *Subjective factors*

    (a) Who will take part in the meeting?
    (b) Who could be persuaded/influenced to take part?
    (c) Who could be persuaded/influenced to stay away?
    (d) What do these people think?
    (e) What do they *think* they know?
    (f) What do they *really* know?
    (g) What do they expect?
    (h) Who is likely to be an ally?
    (i) Who is likely to be an opponent?
    (j) Who is likely to be neutral or indifferent?
    (k) How can these people be influenced or guided?

Dangers in presenting to groups. Marketing specialists, particularly of industrial products and processes, always think they know their customers! They treat them as though they were completely rational beings and not susceptible to selling techniques beyond the bald presentation of product and technical features. Evidence to disprove this assumption can be found in Theodore Levitt's article entitled 'Industrial Purchasing Behaviour', *Harvard Business Review*, 1965. Salesmen and all others involved in group meetings and presentations must perceive the roles individuals play in such collective situations, seeking clues in their speech, behaviour to others and external status symbols.

Salesmen can be

1   Information givers or just talkers.
2   Information getters, Listeners.
3   Negative, nervous, afraid.
4   Meek, apologetic.
5   Brash, 'Mr Big', too positive, overpowering.
6   Mature, poised, friendly.
7   Joker, glad-hander, overfriendly.
8   Impulsive.
9   Neutral, friendly.
10 Goodwill order-taker.

Buyers can be

1   Hostile, recalcitrant.
2   Self important: 'Mr Big'.
3   Joker, glad-hander, nervous, apologetic.
4   Silent.
5   Sceptical, suspicious.
6   Slow, methodical.
7   Mature, poised, thoughtful.
8   Impulsive.
9   Mr Average.
10 Over-cautious.

These factors underline the importance of analysing the *attitudes*, the *knowledge*, *role expectations*, *status*, *position*, *personalities*, of all those whom the selling team will meet at a buying group meeting.

N.B. Bear in mind that even people you may know well on an individual basis are likely to adjust the way they behave as individuals to the role they play or are expected to play at a meeting. Beware in particular of the subordinate in a buying group who promises to pursue a certain policy or course of action at a meeting at which his manager or managing director suddenly decides to be present. The power to hire and fire can sometimes result in promises being forgotten and your erstwhile ally turning opponent.

What support is required?

Most group meetings require support and the form this should take must be planned, for example:

1   Agenda.
2   Folders, with background about people, products, etc.
3   Samples.
4   Briefing of staff involved in providing support.
5   Implications of promises made at group meetings. Ensure that the staff upon whom such promises depend can and will be capable of fulfilling them.

Executing the group presentation

Whatever type of group presentation is to be made or meeting conducted with a buyer group, it requires structure throughout to reflect three factors:

1   Recognition by you that your audience as a whole and each individual member of it wants to feel important, be respected and for you to recognise this in your behaviour and conduct.
2   Ability through your words, your actions, your handling of questions and the solutions you propose to show understanding of the customer situation.
3   Creation of trust and confidence in you, in your company and in your solutions.

These factors pose challenging problems when presenting a proposition more formally to a group or to a larger audience. Frequently at the conclusion of a successful round of negotiation meetings, the supplying company is asked to present the proposition agreed to the board of directors of the buying company or to the sales force. In such situations your presentation must be well planned, if it is to be effective; structured around the needs of your audience, if it is to be well received; and offer solutions in *their* terms, if the desired action is to be achieved.

Room	*Audience requirements*	*Meeting agenda*
Size	Notepaper/pencils	Finalise by
Layout	Product information	Circulated
Chairs	Refreshments	
Tables	Samples	*Meeting budget*
Lighting		£ amount
Electrical sockets	*Audience*	Approved
Window blinds	Notified – briefed	

Programme

1 Meeting's objective(s) ....
2 Information to be presented ....
3 Methods ....
4 Visual aids ....
5 Key discussion points ....
6 Handouts – samples ....
7 Possible objections ....
8 Close planned ....
9 Timing ....

Figure 10.1   Meeting planning and format

The listener's point of view

One of the results of the growth in communications, particularly those involving the visual senses, is that people have become accustomed to certain standards of performance from those who address them. They may not agree with what is being said, they may not even be interested, but they cannot fail to notice the style displayed by the speaker. They remember the image long after they have forgotten the content.

The effect is that it is impossible to say nowadays that any form of presentation will do. Right or wrong an audience, whatever its composition, will judge a man's ability and that of his company by the kind of job he does on his feet. This is not to say that the substance of the speaker's proposals is unimportant, rather that the impact is disproportionately enhanced or diminished by the quality of his presentation. You are in a sense only as good as the ideas for which you gain acceptance. There are four categories of speakers:

1 Those who do not bother about what they are going to say or how they are going to say it.
2 Those who 'put on a show', but convey very little.
3 Those whose material is good, but badly presented.
4 Those who have something worthwhile to say and present it well.

The judge of a presentation is the audience. No two audiences are the same. The individuals within an audience differ in their attitude, but whatever their personalities and job responsibilities may be, they all react to presentations. There are certain mental demands which have to be met before they will give their willing acceptance. In addition, they are affected by what they see, what they hear and how they feel. All these can be summarised as the listener's viewpoint, whose basic elements form a sequence from which a speaker can prepare a structure for his presentation.

Thinking sequence

The thinking sequence that the listener's mind follows consists of seven points. A presentation must take note of them all.

1 *I am important and want to be respected.* Each member of the audience wants the respect of the speaker. Without it the speaker is lost.

2 *Consider my needs.* Any proposal is judged by the listener in terms of his own priorities and sense of values. These are determined by what he wants to achieve:

    (a) in his work;
    (b) as a person.

The content of a presentation will have little impact if the listener cannot see that its theme is about improving his lot. In a business context his needs will be concerned with such things as improved profitability, higher sales, lower costs, better industrial relations, etc. He wants to know early in a presentation that the theme is of this type. If so, he will give the speaker his willing attention and interest. Likewise, his final decision will rest on his answer to one question: 'Will my needs be met by these people and their proposals?'

3 *Will your ideas help me?* If his attention and interest have been gained he is keen to know how the speaker's proposals will help him achieve the end results he is looking for. He wants to know what the speaker's proposals will do for him and his company.

4 *What are the facts?* This step in his thinking process arises from the previous one. He wants to know how the speaker proposes to ensure that the promised results are forthcoming. Depending on the situation he may also want evidence that the promised results have been achieved in other cases of a similar nature. He also wants to know his involvement – action to be taken, time commitment, etc.

5 *What are the snags?* It is an integral part of the listener's decision-making process that he should consider possible disadvantages arising from the speaker's proposals. If any come to mind which he cannot see being overcome, he will frequently voice them in the form of objections. In a group situation there is a bigger chance that objections to the speaker's proposals remain unvoiced.

6 *What shall I do?* Provided all previous points have been covered he is now faced with a decision: 'Do I accept or reject these proposals?' In making the choice he will concentrate on his needs, job or personal, and decide accordingly. If he has several sets of proposals to consider, he will prefer the ones which in his eyes best meet his needs.

7 *I approve.* If Points 1 to 6 have been satisfactorily handled from his point of view, he will make a decision in the speaker's favour.

The importance of the listener's point of view

The seven points mentioned above represent the path that the human mind takes before it will give willing approval to proposals. The problem facing speakers, however, is that by nature they have difficulty in presenting their proposals in that kind of sequence and with that kind of emphasis. In many situations where proposals are being presented the speaker is concentrating on his company and his ideas while the audience is more interested in what they want to achieve. Consequently the audience loses interest, their attention wanders, and they reject both the proposals and the speaker.

By structuring the presentation around the listener's point of view the speaker can go a long way to gaining the audience's attention and interest, persuading them of the value to them of his proposals, meeting their objections, and drawing them to a conclusion in his favour.

Other considerations

When presented with proposals the human mind not only thinks along certain lines, it is affected by what it sees and hears. To a lesser extent it is affected by sensations of touch, taste and smell. In formal presentations *sight* and *hearing* are of the most concern to a listener.

Sight. Listeners react to their first visual impact of you as a speaker. They expect your dress, facial expressions, and gestures to match their mood and the content of your presentation. They look for signs of confidence. Consider the position from the listener's viewpoint. He sees: (a) *How you are dressed.* Are you dressed up in bizarre clothes which will distract your audience from what you say to them? Try and dress neatly and like the group you will be with. (b) *Your mannerisms.* Always be yourself, but avoid distracting mannerisms. Some speakers wave their arms up and down whilst talking, like an Armenian shopkeeper. Gestures should be controlled, few and powerful, and used to emphasise specific points.

Eye contact. Listeners find it much easier to concentrate on and take greater interest in the things they can see. But what they look at must be *understandable*, *simple* and *professionally* handled. They have greater confidence in a speaker who looks at them. Keep in touch with your audience by looking at them.

Hearing. There are two major differences between a public presentation and a normal conversation. During a conversation you can ask your listener if he understands what you have just said, or alternatively he can ask you to repeat something if he did not hear you or understand. But in a public presentation this is not always possible or there may not be any interruptions. So you have to make sure that you get your message across and understood *the first time*. For these reasons, remember the following points:

1   Speak louder than you would in normal conversation. Adapt the scale of your presentation to the size of the room or hall and to the size of your audience so that everyone *hears* you.
2   Always make sure you pronounce words distinctly and emphasise the last words in each sentence. Inexperienced presenters have a habit of fading at the end of each sentence. If

it contains the most important part of your message and no one hears you your presentation has failed.

3 Audiences expect you to speak in language they can understand. Avoid jargon which might confuse people.
4 Don't speak too fast.
5 Vary the pace and vary the pitch of your voice to maintain people's attention and interest.
6 Use *pauses*. Nothing is more effective in a presentation than the pause. It gives the audience time to digest what you have just said or shown, and you time to pick up the substance of your next point. It holds an audience expectant at what you will say next.
7 People dislike having to concentrate on a presentation that is read.

Conclusion

Success in all formal presentation is founded upon understanding the listener, looking at what is *said* and *shown* from his point of view and endeavouring to meet it. Good ideas, however sound they may be, will not stand alone. They have to be presented *attractively*, *clearly* and *persuasively*. This means combining a listener-based structure with presentational skills so that your whole presentation achieves its objective.

Presentation planning

Why prepare?

Presentations are selling situations. They are also unnatural social relationships because:

1 The speaker has usually sought out his listeners.
2 He wants them to act in his favour.
3 He may have to replace their ideas with his own.
4 Additionally, the speaker feels out on his own.

These problems create tension, which makes the speaker act out of character by talking too rapidly, avoiding eye contact with his audience, concentrating on his ideas rather than on the audience's needs. Planning helps to reduce tension and ensures an audience-orientated presentation based on 'your requirements' rather than 'our proposals'.

What should you prepare?

Since planning is simply the thinking process that precedes purposeful action the first thing is to choose *your objective*. This can be a long-term objective covering a series of presentations or a single objective for one session. Having got your objective you can then move to a structure for the presentation proper. For simplicity this structure should be based on the listener's point of view and divided into three main parts, the *beginning*, the *middle*, and the *end*.

Listener's point of view		*Preparation points*
1 I am important and want to be respected. 2 Consider my needs.	Beginning	1 Getting attention. 2 Building rapport. 3 Statement of theme: audience needs.
3 Will your ideas help me? 4 What are the facts? 5 What are the snags?	Middle	1 Points to be made. 2 How they will benefit the audience? 3 Support material: examples; third party references; visual aids. 4 Possible audience objections: answers.
6 What shall I do? 7 I approve.	End	1 Résumé of theme. Audience needs. 2 Summary of points. 3 Closing words: commitment.

How does a structure help?

Apart from reducing tension and ensuring an audience-orientated presentation, a structure has other important advantages for a speaker:

1 It enables the audience to follow easily, because it is based on an initial outline of the theme, followed by development of that theme, and concluded by a summary of the theme, and the points made, with a request for action.
2 To ensure every mental demand by the audience is covered.

3　　It provides a framework to fall back on if the audience leads the speaker astray.

4　　It provides a disciplined and logical basis on which the speaker can plan his presentation.

The needs of your audience

Sit down at your desk with pencil and notepad and imagine you are already in front of your audience. Ask yourself several questions:

1　　Who are they?
2　　What are their needs as businessmen; as individuals?
3　　How much do they already *know* about the subject?
4　　What do they *need to know* that I can tell them?
5　　What are their backgrounds, culture, level of intelligence?

Preparing your notes

One of the most important skills to develop is setting down what you want to say in notes, to which you can refer easily; and not become the prisoner of a sheath of closely written material, and with the eyes glued to this not holding the attention of your audience. For a complicated talk write out what you plan to say in detail. Then select the key sentences or words that summarise each section and put these either on to cards or into check-list form on paper. Then take your notes and not your lengthy first draft with you; the notes will be easy to refer to without making you their prisoner.

Conducting the presentation: the beginning

Objectives

At the start of your presentation you have to achieve three objectives:

1　　Gain the undivided *attention* of your audience.
2　　Build *rapport* between you and your audience.
3　　State the *theme* in terms of the needs of your audience.

How do you achieve each of these objectives?

Methods

1　　*Objective: To gain the undivided attention of your audience.* Before you start speaking the first impact you make on your audience will be through your appearance and manner. Audiences tend to make quick judgements on first appearances. It is important to:

(a) *Stand up straight* in a comfortable stance with your feet slightly apart.
(b) *Look at your audience* in a confident manner. It helps if you have learned your opening sentences by heart so that you do not at the very outset, when you want to hold your audience's attention, bury your head in your notes.
(c) *Talk louder than is necessary for normal conversation.* You have to make instant impact when you speak, so your voice must come out more boldly than you would pitch it in normal conversation.

When appropriate drama, curiosity, a story, a check-list, or questions can be used to attract audience attention, for example:

Dramatic openings. Dame Agnes Weston, who will always be remembered by seamen for her work in collecting money for the Missions to Seamen, often found herself making appeals for money in church halls. If, when she was about to speak, she felt the audience needed galvanising, she would deliberately knock over the lectern which was conveniently placed near her foot. The crash as it hit the floor brought everyone to the edge of their chairs and also woke those asleep!

Another excellent use of drama was used to show the value of training: 'Yesterday a plane, in which my wife was one of the 120 passengers, crash-landed at Heathrow Airport. My wife and her travelling companions owe their lives to the thousands of pounds spent on training the pilot of that aircraft who knew in that moment of crisis, when the undercarriage failed to operate, how to bring the aircraft into land with the greatest chance of saving the lives of those on board. In that moment his training "paid a massive dividend".'

Curious openings. Audiences are always fascinated by the curious. Here are some examples: A salesman selling rock-drills used to carry with great difficulty into the room where he was invited to make his presentation a huge leather bag. From this he would take a massive piece of rock, in silence placing it on a piece of cloth on the table, visible to his audience and then begin: 'Gentlemen, you see before you a piece of the hardest rock in the world. It is found in Jersey. Our rock drills are the only ones made that will break it.'

A pension insurance broker, presenting his scheme to a board of directors, took off the wrist-watch he was wearing and with great ceremony placed it in a glass full of water saying: 'On the back it says "this watch is waterproof". Let us see if the maker's guarantee stands up to the test of its promise. It is about the guarantees behind the pension scheme you are considering today that I want to talk.'

A story opening. A short, interesting story, well told and containing the message you want to convey, or which is linked to the theme of your presentation, can focus attention. Asked to explain 'why marketing is necessary' a sales director began: 'My company once sent me to America and I travelled to New York on the liner Queen Mary. It was at the height of the season, yet the ship was barely half full of passengers. As I puzzled over this on a walk round the deck on the first day out from Southampton, I glanced up into the sky and saw two aircraft winging their way in the same direction as this great ship. And then the penny dropped: overhead flew Queen Mary's erstwhile passengers and presumably her profits. That convinced me that marketing is necessary – that we need to look at tomorrow and ask ourselves how will we stay in business?'

A check-list. Another effective opening is to use a check-list which then becomes the framework of your subsequent presentation, for example: 'Gentlemen, you state that first you need to increase profitability – this scheme will help you do so. Second, you need the security of on-going business – this will give you it. Third, you want to be linked with a successful product – you can be.'

2   *Objective: To build rapport between you and your audience.* A part of the secret of any successful presentation lies in the feeling of oneness between you and your audience. Your audience must warm to you. Never let it be said of you: 'He had everything except one thing. Nobody believed he believed.' Depending on the circumstances, one or more of the following will help build rapport.

(a) *Compliments.* If your audience belong to a company that has achieved something notable you can express your admiration or compliment on it. But compliments paid must be *genuine* and *specific*. Anyone can offer empty praises.
(b) *Mention a common interest.* If you and your audience have things in common these can be mentioned. They can be either *social* or *business*, e.g. 'Gentlemen, as an engineer it is a great pleasure today for me to be amongst professional colleagues'.
(c) Demonstrate your competence, without boasting.
(d) Radiate enthusiasm – it will make your audience enthusiastic.

In your tone of voice, the occasional smile, you can bring a warmth to your presentation which is catching.

3   *Objective: To state the theme in terms of the needs of your audience:*

(a) This is very important because it sets the tone of the whole presentation. For maximum impact the theme should be stated, where possible, in terms of audience needs, for example, addressing a company's top management: 'With competition in your industry becoming stronger and the pressure on profit margins increasing every day, the effectiveness of the people in your marketing team is crucial to your success. It is about their performance and how it can be improved that I wish to talk to you today.' *Not:* 'I'd like to talk about our ideas on marketing training.' In short, if they don't understand what the subject means to them they will lose interest.

(b) If the presentation is going to cover several points it is helpful to mention them at the beginning so that the audience knows what they can expect.

(c) If it is a 'cold' presentation, where the speaker has little knowledge of the needs of his audience, he will have to probe for them by questions until he has agreement on what they are looking for. He can then structure his talk accordingly.

The opening of a presentation sets the scene for everything that follows. The speaker wants his audience to have confidence in him, he wants their undivided attention, he wants to establish common objectives. Above all he wants them to believe that he has something that they will want to know. To achieve these things he has to appear confident, enthusiastic and keen to help them. Above all else, remember this golden rule when preparing your opening words: if you don't strike oil in the first three minutes stop boring.

Conducting the presentation: the middle

Objectives

1   To present the proposals in detail.
2   To have each point accepted.
3   To keep attention.
4   To prevent or handle objections.

Methods

1 *Objective: To present the proposals in detail.* By this time the audience will know the theme of your presentation, and, if it has been stated in terms of their needs, they expect to be informed of the ways in which you propose to meet them.

For the sake of clarity and to aid acceptance it is best to take one point at a time and deal with it before moving on to the next. This can be done in two ways, depending on the subject matter. Either: (a) take one of the audience needs at a time and present the ideas you have for meeting that need; or (b) take each of your ideas at a time and show how it meets their needs. When the subject matter permits, it is better to structure the presentation around audience needs because these are the things uppermost in their minds.

2 *Objective: To have each point accepted.* Acceptance of your points depends on their being understood, seen to be of value in that they will produce a desirable result, known to be valid, and agreed.

(a) *Understanding* can be achieved by:

    (i)   Using language familiar to the audience, avoiding jargon.
    (ii) Explaining ideas by using similes, or going into detail.
    (iii) Using actions or gestures.

Always make sure that an action or gesture does help to communicate the point you are making. To extend both arms to indicate massive size will be effective if you have not used this gesture before. If you have been waving them about all the time then it will not. Leaning forward on the desk from which you are speaking and then stating a serious point can be most effective if your audience has so far not seen you do this.

    (iv) Giving demonstrations.

Nothing directs the attention of an audience from one point to another so surely as a physical demonstration, or showing a piece of equipment. But always: be prepared; practise in advance what you propose to do or show; take your time; tell your audience what you are going to do before you start, and give your reasons for doing it.

For example, an accountant was asked to speak to a group of sales staff about money and what gives it value. He strode into the room carrying a large sack on his shoulder. Then he asked two or three members of the audience to check all the doors in the room and lock them. Assured that all the doors were locked he began: 'In this sack is £10,000 in used £1 notes. I am going to empty them all on to the carpet like this (he then did just that). Now any one of you could help yourselves to fistfuls of these notes. But as long as the doors leading from this room to the outside world where you could spend that money remain locked, those notes are just bits of paper without value.'

(v) Using visual aids.

Like demonstrations, visual aids, skilfully introduced, can convey information and convince audiences. Keep in mind some basic rules about visual aids: uniformity of size is preferable; readability from the back of the room is necessary. Always go to the farthest point in the room and check that what you are showing can be *seen* and *understood* by everyone. If your visuals are not uniform in size then you must carry out this check for each one you propose showing.

Avoid too much detail on one visual aid. Whether it is a chart or a slide, keep information to about *four* lines and make letters three inches high. Sketches, pictures or diagrams linked to words convey your visual message more effectively. Keep numerical information on charts to the minimum. People cannot remember it. Use as few words as possible so that each one makes impact.

Don't apologise for your visuals; just make sure they are good. Keep them hidden until needed. If you are showing a series of charts, then have the top one covered by at least two thicknesses of plain paper; and interleave between the others you propose showing. This avoids the danger of the outline of your visual aids being seen through the flimsy chart paper that is sometimes supplied.

Here is another tip for when you want to write in free-hand three or four key points on a flip-chart; and you are not too good at keeping them in your head or you would like to illustrate a point by means of a diagram and are not sure that you can reproduce it without an outline. Take an HB pencil and very faintly draw on to the flip-chart paper the drawing you want to reproduce; or if it is three/four key points you want to write boldly in magic marker pen, then faintly write in pencil the words in the top right-hand corner of the flip-chart. From a distance your audience will not see or be aware of your self-prepared prompters. From your point of view they provide you with the guides you need without having to rush back to your notes all the time. Number each visual you propose showing and place the relevant visual-aid number beside the points in your notes where you want to show each one (see Figure 10.3).

Allow your audience to note your visuals without distraction. So many speakers ruin the impact of their excellent visuals by competing with them. A picture is worth a thousand words. Show each one and *shut up* whilst your audience take in what you want to communicate.

Remove your visual aids when they have served their purpose. This rule is broken by so many speakers. Overhead projectors are left on: flipcharts with pictures on them, a model remains visible to the audience when the speaker has moved on in his presentation to deal with points totally unrelated to what these visual aids are saying. The result is that the attention of some members of the audience is distracted, and if the speaker is becoming boring, often the important things he wants to say are missed. Afterwards he blames the audience if they do not react as he had hoped. *As always the onus of getting your message across is on you as the communicator.*

Beware of handing out visual material during a presentation. If you want your audience to take away with them a visual reminder of what you have said, it is better to keep such material to the end rather than hand it out in the middle of your talk. Interesting brochures, photographs, diagrams, can often prove more absorbing than a speaker!

(b) *Acceptance* of the value of your proposals is vital. To achieve it: (i) tell your audience what your ideas will do for them: in their jobs; as individuals; or (ii) what your ideas will do for other people in whom your audience are interested, their staff, distributors, superiors, colleagues, customers, shareholders.

The audience wants to know what your ideas will do *in terms of what they want done.* For example, if they want to be certain that your equipment can easily be operated by semi-skilled labour, it is timewasting to emphasise that it fits into a small space thereby increasing production per sq ft. Therefore, if you want your proposals to be desirable to your audience: (i) select the results they will get that fit in with their need; (ii) arrange the sequence so that one result logically leads to another, so that eventually their need is met.

(c) *Validity* of your points may be questioned, albeit mentally, by your audience, especially if your proposals are new to them. Points can be proved by quoting examples of other cases where they have worked. When quoting these examples, or when referring to third parties who have adopted your ideas: (i) don't start with such references; instead, use them to support arguments you have already made; (ii) ensure that the company or people to whom you refer are respected by the audience; (iii) ensure that the circumstances in both cases are sufficiently similar to make your point acceptable; (iv) tell your audience the desirable results the third party obtained.

(d) *Agreement* on the part of your audience is not always visible. Blank silence can imply agreement, disagreement, bewilderment, or boredom. You need agreement on each point before moving on to the next one. It is useful to check it by: (i) constant observation of their facial expressions; (ii) asking questions, if their facial expressions create doubt, e.g. 'are you satisfied that you will have a quality image by using this design?'

3 *Objective: To keep attention.* It is usually in the middle of a presentation that attention declines. To keep it at a high level:

(a) keep telling them what your ideas mean to them;
(b) keep their eyes occupied by using visual aids, demonstrations, etc.;
(c) where possible give them something to do;
(d) quote examples, stories, etc.;
(e) maintain your enthusiasm;
(f) involve them where possible.

4 *Objective: To prevent or handle objections.* In formal presentations the audience is just as likely to think of objections as an individual would in a face-to-face situation. The main difference is that objections are less frequently voiced in formal presentations. It is therefore important that possible objections are considered in advance by the speaker and answers to them woven into his presentation. For example: 'Of course, the initial cost is high, but all the evidence shows that the return far exceeds that of other methods. For example, . . .'

If objections are voiced, the objector wants his views acknowledged by the speaker and answered sympathetically. It pays a speaker to handle objections by:

(a) pausing – this gives him time to think and prevents the temptation to crush the objector with a snappy rebuttal;
(b) acknowledging that the objector has a point, e.g. 'yes, that is an important consideration';
(c) answering by concentrating on what the objector wants.

If the objection is unclear, clarify it by getting the objector to explain what he means.

In many presentations, the middle is the part least remembered, the part where attention is lost, where credibility falls, where objections arise, and where rejection sets in. If the beginning has been good, the middle should be even better. Remember to:

(a) take one thing at a time;
(b) keep emphasising what that point means to them;
(c) keep their attention with visual aids, examples, stories, involvement, etc.;
(d) conclude each point before moving on to the next.

Conducting the presentation: the end

Introduction

1 No matter how long a presentation has lasted, no matter what the subject is, the audience expects it to end on a high note. If it has been good at the beginning, better in the middle, it deserves to be best at the end. If it has been a battle, this is your last chance to make a good impression.
2 The end is where all the threads need to be joined together and all your presentational skills combined to produce a climax that leaves the audience impressed, convinced, and eager to act in your favour.

The psychological barrier

Many speakers feel uncomfortable at having to conclude a presentation. They fight shy of asking for a commitment. Yet a commitment is what they want. They fight shy because they are afraid of getting a rejection and they prefer to leave things open. Such an attitude is understandable, but weak. The audience expects the speaker to draw conclusions from his presentation. He should do so, and confidently ask for a commitment because a commitment is in their interest as well as his.

How to conclude a presentation

1 There are several techniques for this, but in every presentation the speaker should be concentrating on the needs of his audience when he winds up, so that their minds are being focused on their objectives rather than his.
2 From a structural point of view it helps to:

(a) Refer back to the theme – audience needs.
(b) Summarise the points you have made.
(c) If presenting a plan of action, state it in an orderly fashion. Don't leave the audience with a bundle of generalities.

3   Asking for a commitment can be done by using one or more of the following methods:

(a) Direct request, e.g.: 'Can we take it then that you will want to go ahead?'
(b) Command, e.g.: 'Take my advice, adopt this campaign, and let the sales pour in.'
(c) Alternatives, e.g.: 'As you have seen, your problem can be solved by a comprehensive plan which will be ready in three months or by a gradual process starting now and phased over six months. Do you prefer to start now or wait for the comprehensive plan to be ready?'
(d) Immediate gain from immediate decision, e.g.: 'As you know, your competitors have been ominously quiet during the past year and it is believed that they are about to launch a new product at any time. To protect your share of the market, I suggest you start the campaign now and make things as difficult for them as possible.'
(e) Summary, e.g.: 'You want equipment which will reduce your production costs by a minimum of ten per cent. It must be compatible with the equipment you wish to retain and must be fully operational within six weeks from your order being placed. Taking all these points into consideration your best approach will be to purchase our equipment because it will give you what you want.'

Conclusion

1   The end of a presentation should appear to be a logical development from what has previously been said.
2   Asking for a commitment from the audience does not mean that a favourable one will be forthcoming. Action will only result if the rest of the presentation has been audience-orientated all the way through. A rough check of its audience-orientation is to note the number of times 'you' and 'your' are used compared with 'I', 'we' and 'our'.
3   To ensure that your message gets across, remember the phrase: 'Tell 'em what you're going to tell 'em. Tell 'em. Then tell 'em what you've told 'em.'

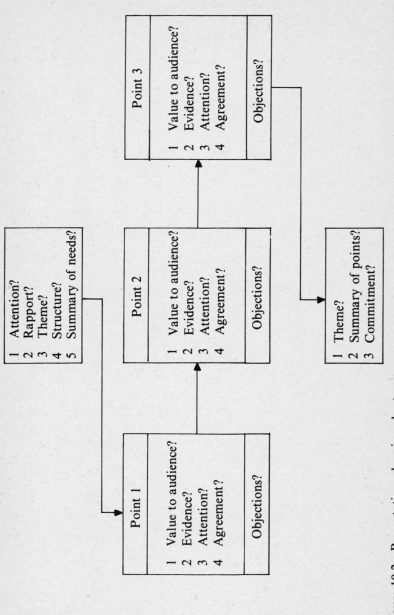

Figure 10.2   Presentation planning chart

1 The title of my talk is...

2 The objective(s) of my talk is/are ....

....

3 Who am I talking to?...

4 What are their *needs*?..

5 *Opening words?* (how am I going to gain their *attention*?)

....

6 *Middle?* (how am I going to maintain their interest?) do I need

.... charts or

.... props?

7 *Prevent objections?* (what objections will there be; how will I identify, acknowledge, handle/answer?) ....

....

....

8 *Close?* (how will I end my talk?) ....

   (a) by summarising?...

   (b) by a story?..

   (c) by three-step formula?..

   (d) by asking for action?...

   (e) by assigning a task?...

   (f) by alternatives?..

....

....

....

Remember to:

(a) smile;

(b) keep eye contact with your audience;

(c) start good, get better as you end;

(d) end on a high note;

(e) write your talk as a check-list;

(f) keep your visuals simple;

(g) stand still.

Figure 10.3   Effective speaking plan

DO...	DON'T...
1 Get your suit pressed.	1 Write your talk as an essay.
2 Dress as the group does.	
3 Look like an expert.	2 Read your talk.

DO . . .	DON'T . . .
4 Get your back to wall or curtain.	3 Talk to your notes.
5 Be yourself.	4 Have distractions behind you.
6 Write your talk as check-list.	5 Talk to your visuals.
7 Smile from time to time.	6 Talk to the blackboard.
8 Talk louder than normal.	7 Walk up and down.
9 Keep eye contact.	8 Lean on the lectern.
10 Face your audience.	9 Fidget with yourself.
11 Stand still.	10 Play with your clothes.
12 Stand erect.	11 Smoke.
13 Stand slightly on your toes.	12 Use the same gesture continually.
14 Lean forward a bit.	13 Compete with distractions.
15 Leave your spectacles on or off.	14 Compete with your own material: if you pass an item out to be looked at stop talking till it has been examined by all.
16 Use variety of gestures.	
17 Tell 'em what you are going to tell 'em.	
18 Then tell 'em.	15 Stand in front of a window.
19 End by telling 'em what you told 'em.	16 Wear clothes that distract attention from what you are saying.
20 Get a good ending.	
21 Keep visuals covered till you need to show them.	17 Fidget with your notes.
22 Remove visuals when they have served their purpose.	18 Overrun your allotted time.
23 Finish before you are expected to.	

Figure 10.4   Effective speaker's do's and don'ts

11 Developing negotiating skills

This workbook has been written with the aim of setting down guidelines and proven techniques which all of you who negotiate business for your companies will find helpful in developing your knowledge and sharpening your skills, so that you can be more successful in your negotiations, achieve more profitable business to the benefit of your company and of yourself, and last but not least enjoy refining the art of negotiating.

Little has ever been written about how to negotiate, despite the fact that, like selling, it is an art that has been practised down through the recorded history of mankind. And so for some of you who have read this book it may simply confirm what you have almost instinctively been doing when faced with what you intuitively recognised and have responded to as negotiating meetings although until now you may not have used such terminology. For you, please use this workbook as a means of recording alongside the techniques described, your own approaches, stances, techniques, and those ideas you have adopted and which have succeeded, so that you can repeat them when the need arises again.

Some of you, having read this workbook, will find it comparatively easy at once to develop and apply successfully the techniques recommended. But others, and you will probably be the majority, will ask how one can be trained to develop knowledge and skills so as to become an effective and successful sales negotiator?

You may, on the other hand, be the sales director of a small company responsible for negotiating some of the most important and profitable parts of your company's business. Or you could be the national accounts manager or one of a team of key account executives in a bank or a large company, or even a public utility.

External courses

For the one man or woman in a business who is responsible for key account negotiation, and where it would be expensive or impractical to have an individually tailored programme, there are external courses

Questions	Answers			
	Knowledge needs	Skills needed	Attitudes needed	Level of expertise
1 What do I need to know and understand about sales negotiation?				
2 What must I be able to do?				
3 What are the circumstances in which I must be able to do it?				
4 What standards of knowledge and skills must I reach to be able to conduct negotiations successfully?				

Figure 11.1   Negotiating skills: personal training needs analysis

specifically designed to develop *sales negotiating skills and related financial knowledge*. Your choice must be made with care because otherwise you may find yourself sitting down with a group of delegates bent upon how to negotiate with trade unions! So here are some guidelines to help you make the right selection (see Figure 11.1).

1 *Define training objective*

    1   What do I need to know and understand about sales negotiation?

    2   What must I be able to do? For example, read a balance sheet, work out break-even charts, prepare and conduct negotiation meetings.

    3   What are the circumstances in which I must be able to do it? For example, negotiate with buyers, intermediaries, directors, government bodies, etc.

    4   What standards of knowledge and skills must I reach to be able to conduct negotiations successfully?

This personal training needs analysis will help you to assess the objectives and content of any course you review much more effectively. Above all it will help you to pinpoint and answer *what you must be able to do at the end of the course.*

2 *Send for information about courses to develop negotiating for profit skills*

Check with the course organisers:

    1   Who actually runs the programme? What are their qualifications as key account negotiators, in finance and above all as trainers? Have they been trained to train?

    2   Which companies have used the course regularly?

    3   Ask the course organisers for the names, positions and telephone numbers of at least three people who have attended the course in the last six months and to whom you can speak about the programme and its effectiveness in *developing skills*.

To save you time, here is a source of information and impartial reference about such courses which will save you searching:

Management Courses Index
Regent House
54–62 Regent Street
London W1
Tel. no. 01–439 4242

3   *Choose a suitable programme and attend it*

4   *Decide what follow-up action is necessary after attending a course*

How are you going to ensure that the time and money invested in attending a training course on sales negotiation yields a worthwhile return? Obviously by applying the techniques learnt on the job. But try and measure improvement if you can by self-appraisal. Write down at least ten and, if you can, twenty major prospects with whom you have been in negotiation up to the time you plan to go on the course and with whom you have so far failed to do business. Then when you have carried out detailed negotiations with them all, and in your judgement should have achieved some measurable objectives, add up your successes and failures. Be honest with yourself. Were the successes due to improved technique or were they fortuitous? Were your failures due to you or circumstances beyond your control?

How to structure a company programme/workshop

A great number of fast-moving consumer goods companies, banks and insurance organisations and service companies employ a sufficient number of sales executives involved in major account negotiation to justify designing an in-company programme organised through their own training manager or commissioning a specialist consultant. Here are some guidelines on how a 'negotiating profitable sales' workshop might be constructed. The term workshop is used quite deliberately because it would be just that: it would be conducted in a workshop environment during which a small group of people would absorb new knowledge, examine systems and techniques and then practise and develop using them to the point of skilled application.

Workshop objectives

By the end of the workshop, sales negotiators will have:

1   Developed a knowledge and understanding of the company's financial, business and marketing objectives and their role in helping to achieve them.
2   Developed the knowledge and skills necessary to assess the marketing and financial implications of negotiations and agreements made with customers and suppliers.

3 Developed their skills in their preparation of negotiations, particularly in trading and buying situations.
4 Developed and refined their skills in conducting effective negotiations to the point of practical application on the job, so that both volume and profit goals are achieved.

Content of workshop

Based upon these objectives, the workshop content and material covered would include:

1 *The background to today's market conditions.* The development of the marketing concept; historical growth of marketing methods and organisation structures; product and brand marketing; development of sales organisation structures and methods; changes in the nature and scale of customer purchasing activities.
2 *Controlling the impact of selling activities on company profitability.* The problems of traditional budgetary systems; lack of genuine accountability for discretionary costs; the salesman as the final arbiter of the marketing mix offered to the customer; the dangers of standard discount systems; the relevance of incentive schemes to the salesman's real performance; the impact of costing systems on negotiation.
3 *Negotiation or Selling? Which technique for which situation?* What are the essential differences between negotiation and selling?; selling defined from a supplier's and a buyer's viewpoint; what relationship between supplier and buyer indicates a selling approach?; what relationship indicates the need for negotiation?; how do the two techniques and skills fit together?
4 *Negotiation – the techniques and skills involved.* A framework for viewing and understanding the process; the strategic elements of negotiation; the tactics of negotiation; the psychology of negotiation; negotiations in practice – an audio-visual example.
5 *The implications for the supplier.* Marketing and sales organisation structures; a more accurate approach; budgetary systems for genuine accountability and more precise control; the selection, development control and motivation of negotiators.

Method

The workshop will be designed to allow the maximum time for discussions and questions arising as each subject and session is presented and developed by the workshop tutor. It should be borne in mind that whilst the temptation to use the company accountant to handle the sessions on finance will be strong it should be resisted unless your accountant is a natural teacher. Very few accountants can teach non-financial people finance in a simple way that all will understand.

The bulk of the workshop will be devoted to developing negotiating skills, using as a means of feedback closed-circuit television, so that negotiators can see as well as hear how they conduct a negotiating meeting and with their colleagues' and tutors' comments and analyses develop their skills.

Role-playing

The most effective way to develop negotiating skills is for each sales negotiator attending the workshop to have the maximum amount of time and opportunity to practise the techniques he has been taught. To achieve this in as realistic a way as possible each person attending the workshop should be asked in advance to bring with him the details of two real-life negotiating situations in which he is currently involved where indicative costings have been calculated and submitted to the potential customers. In addition to these real-life commercial situations, the tutor conducting the workshop should prepare a realistic negotiation situation which can be used in the first stage of skill development. This case should be costed and in addition the concessions to be sought and conceded by either side should be itemised, their cost and value. Using this material, the workshop is divided into a buying and a selling group and each side is given the same information and asked to prepare themselves for a negotiation meeting. This meeting is conducted, recorded on closed circuit television, played back and assessed.

Following the preliminary role-playing to familiarise everyone with the way negotiation meetings are prepared and conducted, the workshop is divided off into pairs, each pair taking one by one the real-life negotiation situations they have brought with them and preparing negotiation meetings based on them. Each pair works on *one* situation at a time. The person whose situation is chosen first will give his colleague all the necessary details he requires to understand the current customer position. Then each member at this point prepares how he will conduct the negotiation meeting, the buyer being played by the salesman whose customer situation is being used, his colleague playing the part of the salesman. Both are given time to prepare their respective positions to negotiate. Then each pair role-play their negotiation. The value of using real-life customer details is that they provide dress rehearsals for the actual negotiating meetings each salesman will conduct after the workshop.

Assessing the role-playing

During the role-playing sessions, each member of the workshop carries out at least one assessment of a negotiation meeting to heighten, through structured observation of negotiating techniques, his ability to analyse the cause and effect of relationships that are revealed and developed and how they influence the final outcome. The manner in which the role-playing is conducted is as follows:

Phase 1. The seller leaves the room to enable the buyer to brief the observer(s) and others on the workshop as to how he proposes to conduct his part of the introduction and deal with the point-of-need balance and his ultimate objective. The buyer then leaves the room whilst the seller tells the group how he plans to conduct his part of the introduction and deal with the point-of-need balance and his selling objective(s). Phase 1 then begins and the nominated observer(s) uses a negotiation observation and evaluation sheet, to record his comments on the check-points a shown in Figure 11.3. The tutor will judge and decide with the role-players the effective conclusion of phase 1. Phase 1 is recorded on closed-circuit television.

Phase 2. The phase 2 briefings will follow the same pattern as for the first phase, this time buyer and seller describing their tactics and the concessions they will seek, trade, and their value. The second phase is then conducted and recorded on closed-circuit television and the observer(s) uses the second section of his negotiation observation and evaluation sheet to record his comments on the tactics and concessions of buyer and seller (see Figure 11.4).

At the completion of each negotiation meeting, the participants are given evaluation sheets; then the recorded meeting is played back and participants' and observers' comments made. Finally the tutor summarises the strengths and weaknesses revealed and where improvements in technique are needed.

Length and numbers on workshop

To cover the comprehensive material presented and develop negotiating skills so that they can be effectively applied on the job after the workshop means that numbers attending must be limited. An even number of delegates should attend and the numbers should not exceed eight as the absolute maximum. Figure 11.2 shows the suggested outline for a workshop spread over a period of three days.

Conclusion

The professional salesman or saleswoman of tomorrow will need much more than basic selling techniques to survive and compete successfully in the years ahead for worthwhile profitable business.

Although you may have been trained in using the best and most effective selling aids available so far and these will still be needed, alone they will not be enough to help you to meet the changed markets and marketing conditions in which you will be operating from now on. Buyers of your products and services, like you, cannot afford to be amateurs. They are becoming bigger in their responsibilities but fewer in the number with whom you can do business. They are becoming professionals in financial knowledge and increasingly skilled in negotiating the purchases of supplies and services. So must you.

Figure 11.2   Negotiating profitable sales workshop

Day and time	Activity and timetable

Day one

09.00	Introduction and workshop objectives.
09.20	Background to today's market conditions.
09.45	Controlling impact of selling activities on company profitability
10.30	Break.
10.45	*Financial implications of negotiation*

	1 Volume requirements.	Participative discussion,
	2 Profit requirements.	plus individual and group
	3 Nature of costs:	exercises, and analysis
	(a) fixed costs;	of specific company

Figure 11.2 (continued)

Day and time	Activity and timetable	
	(b) variable costs; requirements. (c) standard costing; (d) marginal costing.	
12.45	Lunch.	
14.00	*Strategy and tactics of negotiation*	
	1 What is selling?	Participative discussion.
	2 What is negotiation?	
	3 Crucial differences.	
	4 Strategies and their purpose.	
	5 Tactics and their uses.	
15.30	Break.	
15.45	*Planning to negotiate*	
	1 Assessing relative needs, strengths and weaknesses.	Participative discussion, plus group and individual exercises.
	2 Identifying areas for negotiation.	
	3 Identifying mutual concessions, their costs and values to both parties.	
	4 Choosing the sequence.	
	5 Assessing likely customer stances.	
	6 Preparing your own stances.	
	7 Setting limits.	
	8 Selecting participants.	
	9 Planning the conduct of negotiation.	
	10 Choosing the location.	
18.00	Break.	
18.30	Dinner.	
20.00	*Group preparation* Working in pairs, delegates will prepare actual situations for subsequent role-playing exercises.	
21.30	Finish.	

Day and time	Activity and timetable

Day two

09.00	*Review of planning exercise* Presentation of each pair of previous evening's preparation for analysis by the group.
10.30	Break.
10.45	*Conduct of negotiation*

	1 Getting the customer to talk.	Participative discussion, with examples.
	2 Identifying stances.	
	3 Identifying the gap between the parties.	
	4 Swapping mutual concessions.	
	5 Keeping cool.	
	6 Summarising points of agreement.	

11.45	*Final preparation* Each pair will complete its preparation for role-playing.
12.45	Lunch.
14.00	*Individual practice* Each pair will practise simulated/real situation, alternately as buyer and salesman. Each situation will be video-recorded and subsequently played back for evaluation by the participants and the rest of the group.
15.30	Break.
15.45	*Individual practice* As above.
18.00	Finish.

Day three

09.00	*Individual practice*
10.30	Break.
10.45	*Individual practice*
12.00	What has workshop achieved? Each participant identifies future action. Summary and future action specified by manager.
12.45	Workshop ends.

Phase 1.   Introduction and point-of-need balance recognition

What relevant background information is uncovered?

How well does each party 'Position' himself in the estimation of the other?

Check-points	Observer comments	
	The buyer	The seller

Clear objective
Well prepared plan
Well prepared facts
Well prepared background
Presentation of
opening stances
Recognition of
need strengths
Encouragement to
other to talk
Recognition of
opposing tactics
Treatment of
exaggeration
Move from opening
to actual stance
Avoidance of being
'concerned'
Recognition of point-
of-need balance

Figure 11.3   Negotiation observation and evaluation sheet: phase 1

Phase 2. Trading concessions

What use is made of negotiation tactics?

How are 'concessions' presented? Are they given or traded?

Check-points	Observer comments	
	The buyer	*The seller*

Tactics:
Overstatement
Understatement
Face–saving
Emotional reaction
Use of trial close
Facial reaction
Bluff
Confidence
Credibility in use
of facts/figures/
third party

Concessions:
What type?
How traded?
What value?

Movement to conclusion
What snag objection?
How overcome?

Conclusion:
Which side of need
balance?

Figure 11.4   Negotiation observation and evaluation sheet: phase 2

Appendix   Preparing for bargaining*

An overview

1   What are the issues on which we are going to negotiate? Which will he raise? Which will I raise?
2   What is the best settlement I can realistically hope for? What is the worst I would be prepared to settle for?
3   What is my overall objective for bargaining?
4   What are the demands/counter-demands he is likely to make? What concessions am I likely to have to give?
5   How much bluff is he likely to employ? How shall I deal with it?
6   What are the demands/counter-demands that I will make? What concessions am I likely to gain?
7   How much room for manoeuvre is likely in our respective positions?
8   Who are the *individuals* who will negotiate against me? Have they a 'style' which I must counter? Have they weaknesses I can utilise?
9   What can I learn from our last set of negotiations?
10   What are my own strengths and weaknesses as a negotiator? How can I exploit the former and minimise the effect of the latter?

Bargaining power

11   Who has bargaining power? Who *needs* the settlement and at what level?
12   What is it in his bargaining position which gives him bargaining power? How can I counter, minimise or nullify it?
13   What is it in my bargaining position which gives me bargaining power? What can I do to increase or maximise it?
14   Is there any specific action I can take which will increase the strength of my position? Or decrease the strength of his?

Bargaining strategy

15   From my analysis of bargaining power, is there a strategy that will

enable me to improve my position before or during negotiation?

16   Is 'pre-negotiation conditioning' appropriate? If so, when and how am I going to do it?

17   What should my first offer/demand be? Should it be 'high' or 'low'? With many facets or few? Does it leave me with sufficient room for manoeuvre?

18   What strategy is he most likely to employ? How can I counter it?

19   What is my opening statement? How can I get him talking on my terms?

20   How can I get movement from him? Can I/should I:
      (a) incorporate a counter-demand?
      (b) trade a 'phoney' concession?
      (c) link issues?
      (d) trade issues?
      (e) threaten or use sanctions?
      What strategy should I employ for the agenda and/or case?

Remember

For each set of negotiations there is a strategy which is *unique*. You must try to find it and 'play' the bargaining accordingly.

The case

21   Am I quite clear in my mind what it is that I am trying to achieve?

22   Have I sorted out the information that I will use in discussion – because it will stand up to counter-argument – from that which I can't use – because it won't?

23   Have I written down the strengths *and* the weaknesses of my position?

24   Have I considered what I am going to say when he talks about these weaknesses and puts forward his own case?

25   Have I listed the benefits for him of accepting my proposal? Equally, have I listed the *unpleasant* consequences for him of accepting it? How am I going to counter these objections?

26   Have I listed the unpleasant consequences for *both* sides if my proposal is not accepted?

27   Have I thought not only about what I am going to say, but also about *how* I am going to say it? To whom? When?

28   Is there a 'central theme' which I might, with profit, employ?

The bargaining team

29   Are we as skilled in negotiation as is possible? Should the team be given training? Or should there be a substitution with another member of the same group?
30   Have we sufficient general knowledge of the topic under discussion and of the issues to date?
31   Have we got our mandate for negotiation?
32   Have we an adequate degree of authority to reach agreement?
33   Who needs to be kept informed of the progress of negotiations? When and how is this to be achieved?
34   Have the roles of the members of the team been agreed? – analyst and recorder as well as negotiator?
35   Can we be relied on to act as a disciplined team rather than as individuals?
36   Have we *agreed* amongst ourselves on the strategy and objectives for the bargaining itself?

Finally in the light of all this preparation ask yourself:

1   Is my overall objective still valid?
2   Is my strategy still appropriate?
3   Is my case the most relevant?
4   Is my team the most suitable?

*We acknowledge with thanks the permission of the BIM and Gerald Atkinson.

Bibliography

There are very few books available to which those who negotiate major sales can refer, but the following have been chosen because they have proved of practical value in the areas of finance and negotiation.

Finance

International Labour Office, Geneva, *How to read a balance sheet*, 1966.

L. Rockley, *Finance for the non-accountant*, Business Books, 2nd edition 1977.

Robert C. Peterson, *Understand Accounting – Fast*, McGraw-Hill Inc., 1976.

Negotiation

Stuart F. Heinritz and Paul V. Farrell, *Purchasing Principles and Applications*, Prentice Hall, 5th ed., 1971.

Gerald Atkinson, *The Effective Negotiator*, Quest Research Publications Ltd, 2nd ed., 1977.

P. D. V. Marsh, *Contract Negotiation Handbook*, Gower Press, 1974.

Daniele Varé, *The Handbook of the Perfect Diplomat*, published privately, first 1929.

Index